SD
363
.A64
1990

Arbor day.

$38.00

DATE			

© THE BAKER & TAYLOR CO.

Our American Holidays

ARBOR DAY

ARBOR DAY

ITS HISTORY, OBSERVANCE, SPIRIT AND
SIGNIFICANCE ; WITH PRACTICAL SELEC-
TIONS ON TREE-PLANTING AND CONSER-
VATION, AND A NATURE ANTHOLOGY

EDITED BY

ROBERT HAVEN SCHAUFFLER

With a New Foreword by
Tristram Potter Coffin

and a New Index

NEW YORK
MOFFAT, YARD AND COMPANY
1909

Republished by Omnigraphics ● Penobscot Building ● Detroit ● 1990

Library of Congress Cataloging-in-Publication Data

Arbor day : its history, observance, spirit and significance : with
    practical selections on treeplanting and conservation, and a nature
    anthology / edited by Robert Haven Schauffler ; with a new foreword
    by Tristram Potter Coffin and a new index.
       p.   cm. — (Our American holidays)
      Reprint. Originally published: New York : Moffat, Yard, 1909. (Our
American holidays)
    Includes index.
    ISBN 1-55888-865-9 (lib. bdg. : alk. paper)
    1. Arbor Day. I. Schauffler, Robert Haven. II. Series.
    SD363.A64 1990
    394.2'68 — dc20

                                        89-43374
                                             CIP

FOREWORD

Robert Haven Schauffler was a well-known musician and music critic. Born in Austria in 1879 of American missionary parents, he came to the United States when he was two. Educated here, he attended Northwestern and graduated from Princeton. Later, he took courses at the University of Berlin and studied cello with the concert stage in mind. From 1906 to 1909 he and his first wife, Katharine Wilson, performed with blind violinist Edwin Grasse as the Grasse Trio. But it was as a critic, and especially as a popularizer, that he was to make his real mark. *Beethoven, the Man Who Freed Music* and its abridgement, *The Mad Musician*, were top-sellers, as were works on Brahms, Schumann, and Schubert. In *Florestan, the Life and Works of Robert Schumann*, he divided the book into two parts, one an easy-to-read biography, the other a critical discussion of the music.

Schauffler was the quintessential Renaissance man. Besides having a career in music, he was a fine poet, good enough that his "The White Comrade" was one of the better known poems of World War I and that his "Scum o' the Earth" was quoted in pre-World War II editions of *Bartlett's*. He was a successful amateur sculptor. He was a tennis champion, winning the national doubles title in Rome at the age of 27, and the Austrian Handicap Doubles when he was 52. He was an editor (of *The Independent*) and a special contributor to *Colliers, Atlantic Monthly,* and *Century,* among others. His bibliography is pages long. But, most of all, he was a lover of books. "I dote upon libraries in general," he once said. And this interest in poking about the stacks, combined with a love of America (he wrote a book called *Romantic America*), produced the famous holiday anthologies.

There are a number of these holiday collections, anthologies with graceful introductions by the editor, and filled with poems, essays, legends, short tales, and bric-a-brac taken from whatever source caught Schauffler's fancy. The authors range from famous figures such as Robert Browning and Emily Dickinson to writers whose names no one recalls today — such as Henry Park Schauffler and Alice Morse Earle. The books are tastefully edited, with a sound knowledge of literature and a sense of what people like, to the result one encounters not only some of the world's finest writing, but such sentimental favorites as Virginia O'Hanlon's letter to the *New York Sun* asking if there is a Santa Claus, and Theodore Roosevelt's Arbor Day letter to American schoolchildren. "Old chestnuts," like Thomas Buchanan Read's "Sheridan's Ride" or George P. Morris' "Woodman, Spare That Tree," are scattered about, especially in those pages which try to catch the general spirit of the holiday: the collection of lullabies for Mother's Day, the section on immortality for Easter.

The reader has to like these books. If one finds an essay or poem dull or not-to-taste, it is a simple matter to page on. Perhaps it is too bad that the volumes, most of which were published before World War I, were not revised by Schauffler to include more twentieth-century material. He lived until 1964; still, that would have meant some good old poems and legends would have had to be crowded out; and, as they stand, they are happy books, so easy to pick up, so pleasant to open at any spot, so full of sentiment. Martin F. Tupper, just the sort of author Schauffler might have discovered in the stacks, wrote: "A good book is the best of friends, the same today and forever." These are friendly anthologies — and they do wear well!

Tristram Potter Coffin
University of Pennsylvania
March 1990

ARBOR DAY LETTER
OF THEODORE ROOSEVELT, PRESIDENT,
TO THE
SCHOOL CHILDREN OF THE UNITED STATES

ARBOR DAY (which means simply " Tree Day ") is now observed in every state in our Union — and mainly in the schools. At various times, from January to December, but chiefly in this month of April, you give a day or part of a day to special exercises and perhaps to actual tree planting, in recognition of the importance of trees to us as a Nation, and of what they yield in adornment, comfort, and useful products to the communities in which you live.

It is well that you should celebrate your Arbor Day thoughtfully, for within your lifetime the Nation's need of trees will become serious. We of an older generation can get along with what we have, though with growing hardship ; but in your full manhood and womanhood you will want what nature once so bountifully supplied, and man so thoughtlessly destroyed ; and because of that want you will reproach us, not for what we have used, but for what we have wasted.

For the nation, as for the man or woman or boy or girl, the road to success is the right use of what we have and the improvement of present opportunity. If you neglect to prepare yourselves now for the duties and responsibilities which will fall upon you later, if you do not learn the things which you will need to know when your school days are over, you will suffer the consequences. So any nation which in its youth lives only for the day, reaps without sowing, and consumes without husbanding, must expect the penalty of the prodigal, whose labor could with difficulty find him the bare means of life.

A people without children would face a hopeless future ; a country without trees is almost as hopeless ; forests which are so used that they cannot renew themselves will soon vanish, and with them all their benefits. A true forest is not merely a storehouse full of wood, but, as it were, a factory of wood, and at the same time a reservoir of water. When you help to preserve our forests or plant new ones you are acting the part of good citizens. The value of forestry deserves, therefore, to be taught in the schools, which aim to make good citizens of you. If your Arbor Day exercises help you to realize what benefits each one of you receives from the forests, and how by your assistance these benefits may continue, they will serve a good end.

THEODORE ROOSEVELT.

The White House, April 15, 1907.

PREFACE

THE recent awakening of a national interest
in the movement toward the conservation of our
natural resources has emphasized the need for· a
collection of literature on all phases of Arbor Day
more modern than the excellent Manual published
by New York in 1889 and more comprehensive
than the many small Arbor Day annuals brought
out by the various states.

The editor has aimed to include in the present
volume the most practical as well as the most
beautiful essays, articles, letters, stories, exercises,
and poems that have been written about Arbor Day,
its history, observance, spirit, and significance, as
well as those on Spring, trees, flowers, and "green
things growing."

The section on Conservation is of especial
timeliness.

INTRODUCTION

ALTHOUGH Arbor Day is one of the newest of our American holidays, its institution is merely the revival of an ancient custom. It is said that the Aztecs always planted a tree when an infant came into the world, and gave it the child's own name. And the old Mexican Indians plant trees on certain days of the year, under the full moon, naming them after their children.

There is a similar custom of long standing in certain parts of rural Germany, where each member of each family plants a tree with appropriate ceremonies at Whitsuntide, forty days after Easter.

Some unknown seeker after truth once discovered in a Swiss chronicle of the fifth century an account of an early and curious institution of Arbor Day. It seems that the people of a little Swiss town called Brugg assembled in council and resolved to plant a forest of oak trees on the common. The first rainy day thereafter the citizens began their work. They dug holes in the ground with canes and sticks, and dropped an acorn into each hole, tramping the dirt over it. More than twelve sacks were sown in this way, and after the work was done each citizen received a wheaten roll as a reward.

For some reason the work was all in vain, for the seed never came up. Perhaps the acorns were laid too deep, or it might have been that the tramping of so many feet had packed the earth too firmly. Whatever the cause, the acorns refused to sprout, and the townspeople sowed the same ground with rye and oats, and after the harvest they tried the acorn planting again — this time in another way — by plowing the soil and sowing the acorns in the furrows. But again the "great oaks" refused to grow; grass came up instead, and the people were disappointed. But an oak grove they were determined to have, so after this second failure a few wise men put their heads together and decided to gain the desired result by transplanting. A day was appointed in October, and the whole community, men, women, and children, marched to the woods, dug up oak saplings, and transplanted them on the common. At the close of the exercises each girl and boy was presented with a roll, and in the evening the grown people had a merry feast in the town hall.

This time the trees grew. The people of Brugg were pleased and satisfied, and instituted the day of tree-planting as a yearly holiday.

Every year as the day came around the children formed in line and marched to the oak grove, bringing back twigs or switches, thus proving that the oaks were thriving, and every year at the close of the parade the rolls were distributed to be eaten in remembrance of the day. This festival still exists and is known as "The Switch Parade."

"The first to call attention in this country, in an impressive way, to the value and absolute need of trees," writes Egleston,* " was that eminent scholar and wise observer, Mr. George P. Marsh, for many years our worthy representative at the courts of Italy and Turkey. His residence in those older countries was calculated to draw his attention to the subject as it would not have been drawn had he always lived in his native land.

"In Europe Mr. Marsh found the governments of Italy and Germany, as well as those of other countries, making active endeavors and at great expense to rehabilitate their forests, which had been depleted centuries before, to guard them from depredation, and, instead of leaving them to be consumed at the bidding of personal greed or recklessness, cherishing them as among their most precious possessions. . . . He found schools, of a grade corresponding to our colleges, established for the special purpose of training men for the successful planting and cultivation of forests. He found the growth of trees in masses and their maintenance reduced to a science, and the management of the woodlands constituting one of the most important departments of state.

" Such discoveries were well calculated to fix his attention upon the very different condition of the

* "Arbor Day: Its History and Observance," by N. H. Egleston.

forests in his own country, and to convince him that the reckless destruction of them then going on here, if not checked, would bring upon this land the same calamities which had befallen countries of the Old World in past centuries, and from which only the most enlightened nations of Europe are now recovering, through the arduous efforts of many decades, and at great pecuniary cost. The result of Mr. Marsh's observations was the publication of a volume entitled 'The Earth and Man,' and to the admirable chapter on 'The Woods,' more than to any other source, perhaps, we are indebted for the awakening of attention here to our destructive treatment of the forests and the necessity of adopting a different course if we would avert most serious consequences, threatening, possibly, more than anything else our material welfare."

The cause of our American trees was taken up and zealously advocated by a number of public-spirited men, prominent among whom was B. G. Northrup who, in the pages to follow, has written so eloquently of Arbor Day's spirit and significance.

But the official father of the movement was J. Sterling Morton, afterward Secretary of Agriculture during President Cleveland's second term. "In 1872," writes Walsh,* "he was a member of the Nebraska State Board of Agriculture, and he offered a resolution setting apart April 10th of that

---

* In " Curiosities of Popular Customs."

year as 'tree-planting day.' There were some members of the board who contended for the name 'Sylvan Day,' but Mr. Morton talked them out of this title. The resolution as finally adopted recommended that the people throughout the state plant trees on the day named, and offered, in the name of the board, a prize of one hundred dollars to the agricultural society of that county which should plant properly the largest number of trees. To the person planting the largest number of trees a farm library worth twenty-five dollars was offered. The board requested the newspapers to keep this resolution before their readers, and the newspapers responded so generously that more than one million trees were planted throughout Nebraska on the first Arbor Day.

"Next year the day was observed with increased interest, and in 1874 the governor officially proclaimed the second Wednesday of April as Arbor Day for Nebraska. The day was named thus by proclamation until 1885, when the legislature designated April 22d as Arbor Day and a holiday. Since that time a provision has been inserted in the Constitution of Nebraska declaring that 'the increased value of lands, by reason of live fences, fruit and forest trees grown and cultivated thereon, shall not be taken into account in the assessment thereof.' In addition to this, Nebraska has enacted many statutory provisions touching upon the planting

of trees. One directs the corporate authorities of
cities and towns to cause shade trees to be planted
along the streets, and empowers the authorities
to make additional assessments for taxation upon
lands benefited by such planting. Another section
of the law provides for the planting of trees
not more than twenty feet apart upon each side
of one-fourth of the streets in every city and
village of Nebraska. Most persons acquainted
with the needs of really valuable shade trees
realize that such trees should be planted a good
deal farther apart than the distance thus indicated by law.

"One result of all this legislation, and of the pre-
miums offered each year by the State Board of
Agriculture, has been the astonishing prosperity
of nurserymen in Nebraska. In the first sixteen
years after Arbor Day was instituted there were
more than three hundred and fifty million trees and
vines planted in Nebraska, and the observance of
the day is still kept up with interest.

"In 1876 Michigan and Minnesota followed suit,
and like action was soon taken in other states. In
1887 the Education Department of Ontario ordered
that the first Friday in May should be set apart by
the trustees of every rural school and incorporated
village for planting shade trees and making flower-
beds in the school grounds.

"New York did not fall in line until 1888,

when, on April 30, the following act was approved
by the governor:

SECTION 1. The Friday following the first day of May in each
year shall hereafter be known throughout this state as Arbor Day.

§2. It shall be the duty of the authorities of every public school
in this State, to assemble the scholars in their charge on that day
in the school building, or elsewhere, as they may deem proper,
and to provide for and conduct, under the general supervision of
the city superintendent or the school commissioner, or other chief
officers having the general oversight of the public schools in each
city or district, such exercises as shall tend to encourage the planting, protection and preservation of trees and shrubs, and an
acquaintance with the best methods to be adopted to accomplish
such results.

§3. The State Superintendent of Public Instruction shall have
power to prescribe from time to time, in writing, a course of
exercises and instruction in the subjects hereinbefore mentioned
which shall be adopted and observed by the public school authorities on Arbor Day, and upon receipt of copies of such course,
sufficient in number to supply all the schools under their supervision, the school commissioner or city superintendent aforesaid,
shall promptly provide each of the schools under his or their charge
with a copy, and cause it to be adopted and observed.

"By a popular vote the pupils of the state schools
of New York decided that the white elm was the
tree and the rose the flower of the state. They are
therefore called upon to do all in their power to
increase the number of both by planting them on
Arbor Day. With this object in view, Central Park
and the big pleasure grounds in the upper part of
the city are thrown open to them. Small parties
of tree planters start from most of the uptown
schools in the afternoon, and go to some nook chosen

by the Park Commissioners to add their tribute to
the day. Songs are sung during the planting, and
the teachers tell the pupils all about the tree they
have planted, how it will grow, and how grateful
its shade will be to future generations. A luncheon
spread in the open concludes the ceremonies.

"A Spanish holiday (*Fiesta del Arbol*) devoted to
tree-planting was evidently copied from our Arbor
Day. It is celebrated annually on March 26th.
The festival was instituted in 1896. The young
King Alfonzo with the queen regent and the ladies
of the court proceeded to some grounds lying near
the village of Hortaleza, about two miles to the east
of Madrid. There he planted a pine sapling. Two
thousand children selected from the Madrid schools
followed his example. Gold medals commemorative of the event were distributed among them.
The inscription runs 'First Fête of the Tree, instituted in the reign of Alfonzo XIII., 1896.' The
schoolboys who planted the saplings are taken
periodically by their schoolmasters to note the
progress of their respective trees, and are encouraged
to foster tree-planting in their country."

When the idea of the new holiday was fully
grasped there arose at once a chorus of enthusiastic
praise of the day and its founder from significant
voices.

"I willingly confess," wrote James Russell Lowell,
"to so great a partiality for trees as tempts me to

respect a man in exact proportion to his respect for them." Boyle O'Reilly spoke of the day's celebration as "one of the loveliest practices of the country and century." "Francis Parkman," notes K. G. Wells,* "congratulated the West on its discovery." And Edward Everett Hale, with the precision characteristic of him, advised the "State to invest a considerable sum annually, from its sinking fund, in forests."

No wonder the land was stirred by the idea. For the observance of Arbor Day holds quite as rich possibilities of spiritual growth as of merely physical development.

It is a symbol of progress. It is the only one of our American holidays which turns its face toward the future rather than toward the past.

But it holds for the youth of our impetuous and youthfully spendthrift land, a lesson far more needed than that of progress — the lesson of economy and unselfish foresight.

Our young cities have too often been ruthlessly sacrificed to a brutal, hideous materialism; and a large number of our city children have never known the beauty of places devoted to "green things growing." To many of them Arbor Day means the awakening of the æsthetic sense and its celebration often arouses a dormant love for nature which may some day sweep them with a rush out of the crowded,

* In " Pieces for Every Occasion."

unhealthy metropolis "back to the soil," where they are needed.

Then, in turn, Arbor Day, by arousing the "barefoot boy" to a sense of those beautiful miracles of the commonplace amid which he lives, and by keeping him in touch with the modern, scientific side of rural life, is a potent factor in keeping him away from the city and in making him a happier, more intelligent, and more effective farmer.

Many more of the blessed influences of the delightful holiday are fully brought out in the pages that follow.

While the important movement for the conservation of our national resources, inaugurated by President Roosevelt, has given Arbor Day a new national significance, it has emphasized the unfortunate character of its name. ⊢ "If the name of Arbor Day," wrote George William Curtis, "may seem to be a little misleading, because the word 'arbor,' which meant a tree to the Romans, means a bower to Americans, yet it may well serve until a better name is suggested."

The name has served us, it is true, from the days when we first awoke to a dim realization of our criminal waste of trees and its perils. Almost four decades ago, when the infant holiday was christened, our whole idea of the conservation of natural resources was to plant a few trees once a year. But that idea was merely a first vague prelude to our present conviction that we must conserve *all* of our natural resources. And to-day the tree that we plant on Arbor Day is — to our larger consciousness — a mere symbol of the larger conservation which must hand down to our children an unimpoverished America.

If, therefore, the young trees of our young holiday are only expressive and highly poetic symbols of the new wave of unselfish foresight in which America is being baptized, would it not be more fitting, more significant and more beautiful if we should rechristen our new festival with the name — CONSERVATION DAY?

February, 1909. R. H. S.

NOTE

THE Editor and Publishers wish to acknowledge their indebtedness to Houghton, Mifflin & Company; Charles Scribner's Sons; Doubleday, Page & Company; Bobbs, Merrill & Company; Mr. David McKay; The Century Company; Educational Publishing Company; Duffield & Company; Mr. Lloyd Mifflin and others who have very kindly granted permission to reprint selections from works copyrighted by them.

CONTENTS

II

SPIRIT AND SIGNIFICANCE

III

PRACTICAL SUGGESTIONS

IV

THE SEASON

V

TREES

CONTENTS

VI

FLOWERS AND LEAVES OF GRASS

CONTENTS

VII

CONSERVATION

VIII

EXERCISES

CONTENTS

I

HISTORY AND OBSERVANCE

A NEW HOLIDAY*

BY GEORGE WILLIAM CURTIS

A NEW holiday is a boon to Americans, and this year the month of May gave a new holiday to the State of New York. It has been already observed elsewhere. It began, indeed, in Nebraska seventeen years ago, and thirty-four States and two territories have preceded New York in adopting it. If the name of Arbor Day may seem to be a little misleading, because the word "arbor," which meant a tree to the Romans, means a bower to Americans, yet it may well serve until a better name is suggested, and its significance by general understanding will soon be as plain as Decoration Day.

The holiday has been happily associated, in this State especially, with the public schools. This is most fitting, because the public school is the true and universal symbol of the equal rights of all citizens before the law, and of the fact that educated intelligence is the basis of good popular government. The more generous the cultivation of the mind, and

*From "The Editor's Study," *Harper's Magazine*, Copyright 1889, by Harper and Brothers.

3

the wider the range of knowledge, the more
secure is the great national commonwealth. The
intimate association of the schools with tree-
planting is fortunate in attracting boys and girls
to a love and knowledge of nature, and to a
respect for trees because of their value to the
whole community.

The scheme for the inauguration of the holiday
in New York was issued by the Superintendent of
Public Instruction. It provided for simple and
proper exercises, the recitation of brief passages
from English literature relating to trees, songs about
trees sung by the children, addresses, and planting
of trees, to be named for distinguished persons of
every kind.

The texts for such addresses are indeed as numerous as the trees, and there may be an endless improvement of the occasion, to the pleasure and the profit
of the scholars. They may be reminded that our
knowledge of trees begins at a very early age, even
their own, and that it usually begins with a close and
thorough knowledge of the birch.

This, indeed, might be called the earliest service
of the trees to the child, if we did not recall the cradle
and the crib. The child rocking in the cradle is
the baby rocking in the tree-top, and as the child
hears the nurse droning her drowsy "rock-a-bye
baby," it may imagine that it hears the wind sighing
through the branches of the tree. To identify the

tree with human life and to give the pupil a personal interest in it will make the public schools nurseries of sound opinion which will prevent the ruthless destruction of the forests.

The service of the trees to us begins with the cradle and ends with the coffin. But it continues through our lives, and is of almost unimaginable extent and variety. In this country our houses and their furniture and the fences that inclose them are largely the product of the trees. The fuel that warms them, even if it be coal, is the mineralized wood of past ages. The frames and handles of agricultural implements, wharves, boats, ships, india-rubber, gums, bark, cork, carriages and railroad cars and ties — wherever the eye falls it sees the beneficent service of the trees. Arbor Day recalls this direct service on every hand, and reminds us of the indirect ministry of trees as guardians of the sources of rivers — the great forests making the densely shaded hills, covered with the accumulating leaves of ages, huge sponges from which trickle the supplies of streams. To cut the forests recklessly is to dry up the rivers. It is a crime against the whole community, and scholars and statesmen both declare that the proper preservation of the forests is the paramount public question. Even in a mercantile sense it is a prodigious question, for the estimated value of our forest products in 1880 was $800,000,000, a value nearly double that of the wheat crop, ten times that of gold and silver, and forty times that of our iron ore.

It was high time that we considered the trees. They are among our chief benefactors, but they are much better friends to us than ever we have been to them. If, as the noble horse passes us, tortured with the overdraw check and the close blinders and nagged with the goad, it is impossible not to pity him that he has been delivered into the hands of men to be cared for, not less is the tree to be pitied. It seems as if we had never forgotten or forgiven that early and intimate acquaintance with the birch, and have been revenging ourselves ever since. We have waged against trees, a war of extermination like that of the Old Testament Christians of Massachusetts Bay against the Pequot Indians. We have treated the forests as if they were noxious savages or vermin. It was necessary, of course, that the continent should be suitably cleared for settlement and agriculture. But there was no need of shaving it as with a razor. If Arbor Day teaches the growing generation of children that in clearing a field some trees should be left for shade and for beauty, it will have rendered good service. In regions rich with the sugar-maple tree the young maples are safe from the general massacre because their sap, turned into sugar, is a marketable commodity. But every tree yields some kind of sugar, if it be only a shade for a cow.

Let us hope also that Arbor Day will teach the children, under the wise guidance of experts, that trees are to be planted with intelligence and care, if they are to become more vigorous and beautiful. A sapling is not to be cut into a bean-pole, but carefully trimmed in accordance with its form. A tree which has lost its head will never recover again, and will survive only as a monument of the ignorance and folly of its tormentor. Indeed, one of the happiest results of the new holiday will be the increase of knowledge which springs from personal interest in trees.

This will be greatly promoted by naming those which are planted on Arbor Day. The interest of children in pet animals, in dogs, squirrels, rabbits, cats, and ponies, springs largely from their life and their dependence upon human care. When the young tree also is regarded as living and equally dependent upon intelligent attention, when it is named by votes of the scholars, and planted by them with music and pretty ceremony, it will also become a pet, and a human relation will be established. If it be named for a living man or woman, it is a living memorial and a perpetual admonition to him whose name it bears not to suffer his namesake tree to outstrip him, and to remember that a man, like a tree, is known by his fruits.

Trees will acquire a new charm for intelligent children when they associate them with famous

persons. Watching to see how Bryant and Long-
fellow are growing, whether Abraham Lincoln wants
water, or George Washington promises to flower
early, or Benjamin Franklin is drying up, whether
Robert Fulton is budding, or General Grant beginning to sprout, the pupil will find that a tree may be
as interesting as the squirrel that skims along its
trunk, or the bird that calls from its top like a
muezzin from a minaret.

The future orators of Arbor Day will draw the
morals that lie in the resemblance of all life. It is
by care and diligent cultivation that the wild crab
is subdued to bear sweet fruit, and by skilful grafting
and budding that the same stock produces different
varieties. And so you, Master Leonard or Miss
Alice, if you are cross and spiteful and selfish and
bullying, you also must be budded and trained.
Just as the twig is bent the tree's inclined, young
gentlemen, and you must start straight if you would
not grow up crooked. Just as the boy begins, the
man turns out.

So, trained by Arbor Day, as the children cease
to be children they will feel the spiritual and refining
influence, the symbolical beauty, of the trees. Like
men, they begin tenderly and grow larger and larger,
in greater strength, more deeply rooted, more
widely spreading, stretching leafy boughs for birds
to build in, shading the cattle that chew the cud
and graze in peace, decking themselves in blossoms

and ever-changing foliage, and murmuring with rustling music by day and night. The thoughtful youth will see a noble image of the strong man struggling with obstacles that he overcomes in a great tree wrestling mightily with the wintry gales, and extorting a glorious music from the storms which it triumphantly defies.

Arbor Day will make the country visibly more beautiful every year. Every little community, every school district, will contribute to the good work. The school-house will gradually become an ornament, as it is already the great benefit of the village, and the children will be put in the way of living upon more friendly and intelligent terms with the bountiful nature which is so friendly to us.

ARBOR DAY*

BY NICHOLAS JARCHOW, LL.D.

It is not long since some of our treeless Western States, desiring to promote the culture of trees, appointed a day early in spring for popular tree planting. But up to 1883 no state had advanced this movement by the institution of an Arbor Day to be celebrated and observed in schools. Ohio was the first state to move in this matter and to interest the schools in this work. Cincinnati's

* Reprinted from the *Independent*.

Arbor Day in the schools in the spring of 1883 will be remembered by all who took a part in the talks and lessons on trees during the morning hours, and in the practical work during the afternoon. The other states of the East, which have all suffered more or less by the wanton destruction of their primeval forests, soon followed in the wake of the Buckeye State, and our own Empire State celebrated for the first time in the spring of 1889 the Arbor Day in the public schools.

Many considered this scheme impracticable for large cities where trees are a rare sight and where no opportunity is given for practical planting. But the logic of events has now removed any doubts and secured a general appreciation of this subject. To every patriotic American this is most satisfactory, as in the public schools should be introduced what ever shall appear in the nation's life. The foundation of the great deeds the Germans have achieved in every discipline of art, science, industries, and even in warfare, is due to the "schoolmaster." And if we train the youth into a love for trees, the next generation will see realized what we scarcely hope to initiate, the preservation of forests not only for climatic and meteorological purposes, but also for their value in the economy of the nation.

Children may not be able to understand the importance of trees in their aggregation as forests; however. they will, if allowed to assemble in a grove or park, be inspired with the idea that trees are one of the grandest products of God when they hear that without them the earth could never have produced the necessaries of life, and that with their destruction we could not keep up the sustained growth of the plants that feed man and animals. There is no more suitable subject for practical oral lessons, now common in most of our schools, than the nature of plants, and especially that of trees and the value of tree-planting. Such lessons occupy only a little time, taking the place of a part of the "Reader." They tend to form the habits of accurate observation of common things which are of vast importance in practical life. These lessons will lead our youth to admire and cherish trees, thus rendering a substantial service to the State as well as to the pupils by making them practical arborists.

Wherever the opportunity is given, children should be encouraged to plant or help in planting a tree, shrub or flower, actually practising what they have learned in the study of the growth and habits of plants. They will watch with pride the slow but steady development of a young tree, and find a peculiar pleasure in its parentage. Such work has not only an educational effect upon the juvenile mind, but its æsthetic influence cannot be overestimated. Tree planting is a good school for discipline in foresight, the regard for the future being

the leading element in this work. Young people
are mostly inclined to sow only where they can soon
reap; they prefer the small crop in hand to a great
harvest long in maturing. But when they are led
to obtain a taste for trees, the grandeur of thought
connected with this important line of husbandry
will convince them that a speedy reward is not always
the most desirable motive in the pursuits of our life,
and is not worthy of aspiring men. For patiently to
work year after year for the attainment of a far-off
end shows a touch of the sublime, and implies moral
no less than mental heroism.

ARBOR DAY IN SCHOOLS.*

BY B. G. NORTHRUP

J. STERLING MORTON, once Secretary of the United
States Department of Agriculture, originated Arbor
Day in Nebraska in 1872. His able advocacy of
this measure was a marvelous success the first year,
and still more each succeeding year. So remarkable have been the results of Arbor Day in Nebraska
that its originator is gratefully recognized as the
great benefactor of his state. Proofs of public appreciation of his grand work I found wherever I have
been in that state. It glories in the old misnomer
of the geographies, "The Great American Desert,"

* Reprinted from the *Independent.*

since it has become so habitable and hospitable by cultivation and tree-planting. Where, twenty years ago, the books said trees would not grow, the settler who does not plant them is the exception. The Nebraskans are justly proud of his great achievement and are determined to maintain its pre-eminence.

Arbor Day for economic tree-planting and Arbor Day in schools differ in origin and scope. Both have been erroneously attributed to me, though long ago I advocated tree-planting by youth, and started the scheme of centennial tree-planting, offering a dollar prize, in 1876, to every boy or girl who should plant, or *help in planting*, five "centennial trees"; still the happy idea of designating a given day when all should be invited to unite in this work belongs solely to ex-Governor Morton. His great problem was to meet the urgent needs of vast treeless prairies. At the meeting of the American Forestry Association, held at St. Paul in 1883, my resolution in favor of observing Arbor Day *in schools* in all our states was adopted, and a committee was appointed to push that work. Continued as their chairman from that day to this, I have presented the claims of Arbor Day personally, or by letter, to the governor, or state school superintendent in all our states and territories.

My first efforts were not encouraging. The indifference of state officials who, at the outset, deemed Arbor Day an obtrusive innovation, was expected and occasioned no discouragement. My last word with more than one governor was: "This thing is sure to go. My only question is, shall it be under your administration or that of your successor?" Many state officials who at first were apathetic, on fuller information have worked heartily for the success of Arbor Day. The logic of events has answered objections. Wherever it has been fairly tried it has stood the test of experience. Now such a day is observed in forty states and territories, in accordance with legislative acts or recommendation of state agricultural and horticultural societies, of the state grange, or by special proclamation of the governor or recommendation of the state school superintendents, and in some states by all these combined. It has already become the most interesting, widely observed and useful of school holidays. It should not be a legal holiday, though that may be a wise provision for the once treeless prairies of Nebraska.

Popular interest in this work has been stimulated by the annual proclamations of governors and the full and admirable circulars to state and county school superintendents sent to every school in the State.

Arbor Day has fostered love of country. It has become a patriotic observance in those Southern States which have fixed its date on Washington's

Birthday. Lecturing in all these states, I have been delighted to find as true loyalty to the Stars and Stripes in them as in the North. This custom of planting memorial trees in honor of Washington, Lincoln, and other patriots, and also of celebrated authors and philanthropists, has become general. Now that the national flag with its forty-five stars floats over all the school-houses in so many states, patriotism is effectively combined with the Arbor Day addresses, recitations and songs. Among the latter "The Star Spangled Banner" and "America" usually find a place. Who can estimate the educating influence exerted upon the millions of youth who have participated in these exercises? This good work has been greatly facilitated by the eminent authors of America who have written so many choice selections in prose and poetry on the value and beauty of trees, expressly for use on Arbor Day. What growth of mind and heart has come to myriads of youth who have learned these rich gems of our literature and applied them by planting and caring for trees, and by combining sentiments of patriotism with the study of trees, vines, shrubs, and flowers, and thus with the love of Nature in all her endless forms and marvelous beauty!

An eminent educator says: "Any teacher who has no taste for trees, shrubs or flowers is unfit to be placed in charge of children." Arbor Day has enforced the same idea, especially in those states in which the pupils have cast their ballots on Arbor Day in favor of a state tree and state flower. Habits of observation have thus been formed which have led youth in their walks, at work or play, to recognize and admire our noble trees, and to realize that they are the grandest products of Nature and form the finest drapery that adorns the earth in all lands. How many of these children in maturer years will learn from happy experience that there is a peculiar pleasure in the parentage of trees, forest, fruit or ornamental — a pleasure that never cloys but grows with their growth.

Arbor Day has proved as memorable for the home as the school, leading youth to share in dooryard adornments. Much as has been done on limited school grounds, far greater improvements have been made on the homesteads and the roadsides. The home is the objective point in the hundreds of village improvement societies recently organized. The United States Census of 1890 shows that there has recently been a remarkable increase of interest in horticulture, arboriculture, and floriculture. The reports collected from 4,510 nurserymen give a grand total of 3,386,855,778 trees, vines, shrubs, roses, and plants as then growing on their grounds. Arbor Day and village improvement societies are not the least among the many happy influences that have contributed to this grand result.

ARBOR DAY'S OBSERVANCE

BY A. S. DRAPER

THE primary purpose of the legislature in establishing "Arbor Day," was to develop and stimulate in the children of the Commonwealth a love and reverence for Nature as revealed in trees and shrubs and flowers. In the language of the statute, "to encourage the planting, protection and preservation of trees and shrubs" was believed to be the most effectual way in which to lead our children to love Nature and reverence Nature's God, and to see the uses to which these natural objects may be put in making our school grounds more healthful and attractive.

The object sought may well command the most thoughtful consideration and the painstaking efforts of school officers, teachers, and pupils in every school district, and in every educational institution and of all others who are interested in beautifying the schools and the homes of the state.

It will be well not only to plant trees and shrubs and vines and flowers where they may contribute to pleasure and comfort, but also to provide for their perpetual care, and to supplement such work by exercises which will lead all to a contemplation of the subject in its varied relations and resultant influences. It is fitting that trees should be dedicated to eminent scholars, educators, statesmen, soldiers, historians or poets, or to favorite teachers or pupils in the different localities.

The opportunity should not be lost, which is afforded by the occasion, for illustrating and enforcing the thought that the universe, its creation, its arrangement and all of its developing processes are not due to human planning or oversight, but to the infinite wisdom and power of God.

Our school exercises, and particularly those of an unusual character, should be interspersed with selections, songs, and acts which will inspire patriotism.

A HYMN FOR ARBOR DAY

BY HENRY HANBY HAY

(To be sung by schools to the time of "America")

God save this tree we plant!
And to all nature grant
  Sunshine and rain.
Let not its branches fade,
Save it from axe and spade,
Save it for joyful shade —
  Guarding the plain.

When it is ripe to fall,
Neighbored by trees as tall,
  Shape it for good.

Shape it to bench and stool,
Shape it to square and rule,
Shape it for home and school,
    God bless the wood.

Lord of the earth and sea,
Prosper our planted tree,
    Save with Thy might.
Save us from indolence,
Waste and improvidence,
And in Thy excellence,
    Lead us aright.

ARBOR DAY

ANONYMOUS

OUR modern institution — Arbor Day — is a public acknowledgement of our dependence upon the soil of the earth for our daily, our annual, bread. In recognition of the same fact the Emperor of China annually plows a furrow with his own hand, and in the same significance are the provisions in the ancient law of Moses, to give the land its seven-year Sabbath, as well as to man his seventh day for rest and recreation. Our observance is a better one, because it calls on all, and especially on the impressible learners in the schools to join in the duty which we owe to the earth and to all mankind, of doing what each of us can to preserve the soil's fertility, and to prevent, as long as possible, the earth, from which we have our being, from becoming worn out and wholly bald and bare. And we do this by planting of any sort, if only by making two blades of grass grow where but one grew before, and by learning to preserve vegetation. We give solemnity to this observance by joining in it on an appointed day, high and low, old and young, together.

HE WHO PLANTS AN OAK

BY WASHINGTON IRVING

HE WHO plants an oak looks forward to future ages, and plants for posterity. Nothing can be less selfish than this. He cannot expect to sit in its shade nor enjoy its shelter; but he exults in the idea that the acorn which he has buried in the earth shall grow up into a lofty pile, and shall keep on flourishing and increasing, and benefiting mankind long after he shall have ceased to tread his paternal fields. The oak, in the pride and lustihood of its growth, seems to me to take its range with the lion and the eagle, and to assimilate, in the grandeur of its attributes, to heroic and intellectual man.

With its mighty pillar rising straight and direct toward heaven, bearing up its leafy honors from the impurities of earth, and supporting them aloft

in free air and glorious sunshine, it is an emblem of
what a true nobleman should be; a refuge for the
weak — a shelter for the oppressed — a defense
for the defenseless; warding off from them the
peltings of the storm, or the scorching rays of arbitrary power.

THE PLANTING OF THE APPLE-TREE

BY WILLIAM CULLEN BRYANT

COME, let us plant the apple-tree!
Cleave the tough greensward with the spade;
Wide let its hollow bed be made;
There gently lay the roots, and there
Sift the dark mold with kindly care,
   And press it o'er them tenderly,
As round the sleeping infant's feet
We softly fold the cradle-sheet;
   So plant we the apple-tree.

What plant we in this apple-tree?
Buds which the breath of summer days
Shall lengthen into leafy sprays;
Boughs where the thrush, with crimson breast,
Shall haunt, and sing, and hide her nest;
   We plant upon the sunny lea
A shadow for the noontide hour,
A shelter from the summer shower,
   When we plant the apple-tree.

What plant we in this apple-tree?
Sweets for a hundred flowery springs
To load the May-wind's restless wings,
When from the orchard-row he pours
Its fragrance through our open doors;
   A world of blossoms for the bee,
Flowers for the sick girl's silent room,
For the glad infant sprigs of bloom,
   We plant with the apple-tree.

What plant we in this apple-tree?
Fruits that shall swell in sunny June,
And redden in the August noon,
And drop when gentle airs come by,
That fan the blue September sky;
   While children, wild with noisy glee,
Shall scent their fragrance as they pass
And search for them the tufted grass
   At the foot of the apple-tree.

And when above this apple tree
The winter stars are quivering bright,
And winds go howling through the night,
Girls, whose young eyes o'erflow with mirth,
Shall peel its fruit by the cottage hearth;
   And guests in prouder homes shall see,
Heaped with the orange and the grape,
As fair as they in tint and shape,
   The fruit of the apple-tree.

The fruitage of this apple-tree,
Winds, and our flag of stripe and star,
Shall bear to coasts that lie afar,
Where men shall wonder at the view,
And ask in what fair groves they grew:
  And they who roam beyond the sea
Shall think of childhood's careless day,
And long hours passed in summer play
    In the shade of the apple-tree.

Each year shall give this apple-tree
A broader flush of roseate bloom,
A deeper maze of verdurous gloom,
And loosen, when the frost-clouds lower,
The crisp brown leaves in thicker shower.
  The years shall come and pass; but we
Shall hear no longer, where we lie,
The summer's songs, the autumn's sigh,
    In the boughs of the apple-tree.

But time shall waste this apple-tree.
Oh, when its aged branches throw
Thin shadows on the ground below,
Shall fraud and force and iron will
Oppress the weak and helpless still?
  What shall the task of mercy be,
Amid the toils, the strifes, the tears
Of those who live when length of years
    Is wasting this apple-tree?

"Who planted this old apple-tree?"
The children of that distant day
Thus to some aged man shall say;
And, gazing on its mossy stem,
The gray-haired man shall answer them:
"A poet of the land was he,
Born in the rude but good old times;
'Tis said he made some quaint old rhymes
On planting the apple-tree."

TREE PLANTING

BY OLIVER WENDELL HOLMES

(Extract from Letter)

THE trees may outlive the memory of more than one of those in whose honor they were planted. But if it is something to make two blades of grass grow where only one was growing, it is much more to have been the occasion of the planting of an oak which shall defy twenty scores of winters, or of an elm which shall canopy with its green cloud of foliage half as many generations of mortal immortalities. I have written many verses, but the best poems I have produced are the trees I planted on the hillside which overlooks the broad meadows, scalloped and rounded at their edges by loops of the sinuous Housatonic. Nature finds rhymes for them in the recurring measures of the seasons.

Winter strips them of their ornaments and gives them, as it were, in prose translation, and summer reclothes them in all the splendid phrases of their leafy language.

What are these maples and beeches and birches but odes and idyls and madrigals? What are these pines and firs and spruces but holy hymns, too solemn for the many-hued raiment of their gay deciduous neighbors?

————

THE CELEBRATION OF ARBOR DAY

BY MONCURE D. CONWAY

(*Extract from Letter*)

IT IS a great pleasure to think of the young people assembling to celebrate the planting of trees, and connecting them with the names of authors whose works are the further and higher products of our dear old Mother Nature. An Oriental poet says of his hero:

> Sunshine was he in a wintry place,
> And in the midsummer coolness and shade.

Such are all true thinkers, and no truer monuments of them can exist than beautiful trees. Our word book is from the beech tablets on which men used to write. Our word Bible is from the Greek for bark of a tree. Our word paper is from the tree papyrus — the tree which Emerson found the most

interesting thing he saw in Sicily.   Our word library
is from the Latin *liber*, bark of a tree.   Thus literature is traceable in the growth of trees, and was
originally written on leaves and wooden tablets.
The West responds to the East in associating
great writers with groups of trees, and a grateful
posterity will appreciate the poetry of this idea
as well while it enjoys the shade and beauty
which the schools are securing for it.

SPRING CLEANING

BY SAM WALTER FOSS

From *The Yankee Blade*

YES, clean yer house, an' clean yer shed,
  An' clean yer barn in every part;
But brush the cobwebs from yer head,
  An' sweep the snowbank from yer heart;
Jes' w'en spring cleanin' comes aroun'
  Bring forth the duster an' the broom,
But rake your fogy notions down,
  An' sweep yer dusty soul of gloom.

Sweep ol' ideas out with the dust,
  An' dress the soul in newer style,
Scrape from yer min' its wornout crust,
  An' dump it in the rubbish pile;
Sweep out the dates that burn an' smart,
  Bring in new loves serene an' pure,

Aroun' the hearthstone of the heart
   Place modern styles of furniture.

Clean out yer moril cubby-holes,
   Sweep out the dirt, scrape off the slum!
'Tis cleaning time for healthy souls;
   Get up and dust! The spring hez come!
Clean out the corners of the brain,
   Bear down with scrubbin' brush and soap,
And dump ol' Fear into the rain,
   An' dust a cozy chair for Hope.

Clean out the brain's deep rubbish hole,
   Soak every cranny, great an' small,
An' in the front room of the soul
   Hang pootier pictures on the wall.
Scrub up the winders of the mind,
   Clean up, an' let the spring begin;
Swing open wide the dusty blind,
   An' let the April sunshine in.

Plant flowers in the soul's front yard,
   Set out new shade and blossom trees,
An' let the soul once froze and hard
   Sprout crocuses of new idees.
Yes, clean yer house an' clean yer shed,
   An clean yer barn in ev'ry part;
But brush the cobwebs from yer head
   An' sweep the snowbanks from yer heart.

A UNIQUE CELEBRATION

From *Journal of Education*

THE most unique celebration of Arbor Day, probably, is that which occurs at Eynsford, England, where some remarkable commemorative tree-planting has taken place.   The observance began in 1897, during Queen Victoria's diamond jubilee, when shade trees were planted in acrostic form, and an orchard of apple trees was set out.   During the South African war the shade trees commemorated the defense of Kimberly, Ladysmith, and Mafeking. In 1902, four years after Queen Victoria's death, trees were planted along the main road as a memorial in acrostic form, expressing Lord Tennyson's line:—

> She wrought her people lasting good.

Since then a quarter of a mile of trees have been planted whose initial letters spell out two lines from Robert Browning's "Rabbi Ben Ezra":

> The best is yet to be:
> The last of life for which the first was made.

In this way the people are drawn to learn the names of many different varieties of trees, so as to identify them at sight and read the couplets from the fifty-two initial letters, for themselves.

ARBOR DAY SONG

BY MARY A. HEERMANS

OF NATURE broad and free,
Of grass and flower and tree,
  Sing we to-day.
God hath pronounced it good,
So we, His creatures would
Offer to field and wood
  Our heartfelt lay.

To all that meets the eye,
In earth, or air, or sky,
  Tribute we bring.
Barren this world would be,
Bereft of shrub and tree;
Now gracious Lord to Thee
  Praises we sing.

May we Thy hand behold,
As bud and leaf unfold,
  See but Thy thought;
Nor heedlessly destroy,
Nor pass unnoticed by;
But be our constant joy
  All Thou has wrought.

As each small bud and flower
Speaks of the Maker's power,
  Tells of His love;

So we, Thy children dear,
Would live from year to year,
Show forth Thy goodness here,
And then above.

CELEBRATING ARBOR DAY

BY WALTER E. RANGER

From *Rhode Island Arbor Day Annual*, 1907

BY AN excursion into the woods pupils may learn, under the direction of their teacher, to identify the most common kinds of trees and gain a more intimate acquaintance with trees. Such an excursion, when practicable, would not be an unfitting feature of Arbor Day observance, and would not necessarily preclude other customary exercises both within and without the schoolroom.

The State Forester has made the following interesting suggestion: "It would seem to me expedient for some of the schools to reserve a shaded corner of the grounds for a small forest nursery — a bed about four feet wide and any convenient length — in which to raise nursery stock for planting shade and forest trees on Arbor Day. Such a nursery could be started on Arbor Day by putting into this bed some tiny seedlings such as may be found at that time under some of the mature trees of beech, maple, oak, ash, pine, and chestnut. Later the nursery could be extended by planting tree-seeds gathered in the following autumn."

The proper observance of Arbor Day is limited neither to literary programme nor to tree planting. Since man's visible works are but an expression of his life, the aim of the school must be the development of virile character, of which good works are the issue. For this end in the training of children and youth, Arbor Day offers the opportunity of fostering the love of natural beauty, awakening an interest in civic improvement, imparting a knowledge of the value of trees, giving instruction in practical forestry, and providing a practical training in tree-planting and related arts. If the children of to-day form the habit of making things look better at school and home, they will later be found active in all efforts for public improvement.

An interesting programme of song and recitation and the making of some spot more beautiful by tree, shrub, or flower are alike means for making impressions of truth and beauty that will endure in the lives of children. For this purpose it is essential that every school convene in its school home on Arbor Day morning and that every child shall have a personal part, however small, in the exercises of the day.

Let Arbor Day be associated with the study of nature throughout the year. Let every school, when possible, have its garden. Keeping the school yard free from rubbish is a way of improvement. For adornment of school grounds the planting of shrubs and vines, as well as trees, may be effective. For the sake of the children every school-house should image God's beauty of field and forest. The future beauty of homestead, school grounds, roadside and public park is now growing in the hearts of to-day's children. Let the school become an ally of the community in all public betterment.

The proper observance of Arbor Day contributes not a little to right civic training. It strengthens the link between the child and nature. In awakening an interest in the life of tree and plant, it inspires kindness, gentle manners, and a fine regard for the rights and well-being of others. It gives a larger love of home and familiar scenes and a deep interest in men and things, which is at the heart of good citizenship.

WHAT DO YOU SEE?

From *Wisconsin Arbor and Bird Day Annual*, 1903

WHETHER we see much or little in nature is determined by the intelligence and training of the mind which interprets what our eyes look upon. Nature is a closed book to many and tells no story of interest and beauty.

The first purpose of the celebration of Arbor Day should be to arouse in children a strong desire to

know more about trees and flowers and animals
about them, and to care more for them.

The teacher who can, on this and succeeding
days, accomplish this purpose, may rest assured
that she has done much to enlarge the life and
increase the happiness of those in her care. Children are always interested in life. It is to them a
source of continual curiosity and wonder.

The intelligent teacher will find it easy but necessary to direct this interest so that it shall result in close
observation and serious study. The materials are
always at hand. Every season presents life in a
new aspect, and in almost infinite variety.

Do not permit the minds of the children to be
diverted from the simple thought of this day.
While it is unquestionably desirable to have the
school-house and grounds cleaned at this season of
the year, this should be done as a preparation for
Arbor Day, not as a part of its celebration. Let
no drudgery turn the children's minds from the full
enjoyment of the day.

The schoolroom should be decorated as tastefully
as possible. For this purpose encourage the children to bring flowers and birds from their homes.
The joyousness and beauty of nature should fill
the schoolroom. Plant some flowers as well as
trees. Even if the school ground is small so that
most of it must be used by the children for a playground, surely some little corner may be found for

a flower bed. The care and growth of these flowers will furnish materials for many an interesting lesson. In Japan, where the great population makes it necessary for the yards about the homes to be very small, the family always finds some little plot for flowers to give a touch of color and beauty to their homes. Those who have visited this far-off land testify how much this adds to the attractiveness of the simple dwellings of the Japanese. The ordinary country school-house needs all the charm that can be added by this inexpensive decoration to make it an attractive home for children. The usual barrenness of it all, the lack of taste in its architecture and beauty in its surroundings, are not likely to cultivate high æsthetic ideals in the youthful minds; and the ideals of childhood must certainly have much influence upon the homes which these same children, grown to men and women, will control later in life. How much a few vines planted on Arbor and Bird Day, or at any other suitable season, will accomplish in rendering the exterior of the school or the home attractive! Flowers, vines and trees, beautifying the school-house and grounds, react and beautify the homes. The interests of children do much to determine the interest of parents. When fathers and mothers find their children enthusiastic in their efforts to render their school-house attractive and pleasant, the homes will sooner or later show the results.

School decoration is almost certain to result in home decoration.

The Arbor Day programme should teach a lesson in kindness to animals. If children become interested in the study of the habits and characteristics of animals, there is little likelihood that cruelty will be practised. As we learn to know animals, we find in them so many qualities that appeal to our sympathies and our interests, that the desire to destroy or harm fades away. The boy who has learned from experience that many wild animals will soon cease to fear him if he does not frighten them, is not likely to continue to injure them, for he will want them to be his friends.

AN ARBOR DAY TREE

UNKNOWN

DEAR little tree that we plant to-day,
What will you be when we're old and gray?
"The savings bank of the squirrel and mouse,
For robin and wren an apartment house,
The dressing-room of the butterfly's ball,
The locust's and katydid's concert hall,
The schoolboy's ladder in pleasant June,
The schoolgirl's tent in the July noon,
And my leaves shall whisper them merrily
A tale of the children who planted me."

WHEN WE PLANT A TREE*

BY OLIVER WENDELL HOLMES

(*Extract from Letter*)

WHEN we plant a tree, we are doing what we can to make our planet a more wholesome and happier dwelling place for those who come after us if not for ourselves.

As you drop the seed, as you plant the sapling, your left hand hardly knows what your right hand is doing. But Nature knows, and in due time the Power that sees and works in secret will reward you openly. You have been warned against hiding your talent in a napkin; but if your talent takes the form of a maple-key or an acorn, and your napkin is a shred of the apron that covers "the lap of the earth," you may hide it there, unblamed; and when you render in your account you will find that your deposit has been drawing compound interest all the time.

PLANT A TREE*

BY LUCY LARCOM

HE WHO plants a tree
    Plants a hope.
Rootlets up through fibres blindly grope;
Leaves unfold into horizons free.

* By special permission of Houghton, Mifflin & Co.

So man's life must climb
From the clods of time
Unto heavens sublime.
Canst thou prophesy, thou little tree,
What the glory of thy boughs shall be?

He who plants a tree
Plants a joy;
Plants a comfort that will never cloy.
Every day a fresh reality,
Beautiful and strong,
To whose shelter throng
Creatures blithe with song.
If thou couldst but know, thou happy tree,
Of the bliss that shall inhabit thee!

He who plants a tree,
He plants peace.
Under its green curtains jargons cease;
Leaf and zephyr murmur soothingly;
Shadows soft with sleep
Down tired eyelids creep,
Balm of slumber deep.
Never hast thou dreamed, thou blessed tree,
Of the benediction thou shalt be.

He who plants a tree,
He plants youth;
Vigor won for centuries, in sooth;
Life of time, that hints eternity!

Boughs their strength uprear,
New shoots every year
On old growths appear.
Thou shalt teach the ages, sturdy tree,
Youth of soul is immortality.

He who plants a tree,
He plants love.
Tents of coolness spreading out above
Wayfarers he may not live to see.
Gifts that grow are best;
Hands that bless are blest;
Plant: Life does the rest!
Heaven and earth help him who plants a tree,
And his work its own reward shall be.

II

SPIRIT AND SIGNIFICANCE

THE HEART OF THE TREE*

BY HENRY CUYLER BUNNER

WHAT does he plant who plants a tree?
  He plants the friend of sun and sky;
He plants the flag of breezes free;
  The shaft of beauty towering high;
  He plants a home to heaven anigh,
    For song and mother-croon of bird
    In hushed and happy twilight heard —
The treble of heaven's harmony —
These things he plants who plants a tree.

What does he plant who plants a tree,
  He plants cool shade and tender rain,
And seed and bud of days to be,
  And years that fade and flush again;
  He plants the glory of the plain;
    He plants the forest's heritage;
    The harvest of a coming age;
The joy that unborn eyes shall see —
These things he plants who plants a tree.

What does he plant who plants a tree?
  He plants, in sap and leaf and wood,

In love of home and loyalty
  And far-cast thought of civic good —
  His blessings on the neighborhood,
    Who in the hollow of His hand
    Holds all the growth of all our land —
A nation's growth from sea to sea
Stirs in his heart who plants a tree.

———

THE SPIRIT OF ARBOR DAY

BY FRANK A. HILL

THE spirit of Arbor Day is that of a deep love for trees — a love that includes their beauty on the one hand and their service on the other. This love has a thousand aspects and a thousand degrees, for the beauty and the service that call it forth are as varied as the trees that grow and the needs of earth and man to which they so admirably minister. There is the beauty of the stately pine, the rugged oak, the graceful elm. There is the service of the fragrant eucalyptus that brings health to the deadly Campagna, of the versatile palm that makes habitable the waste places of the tropical belt, of the humid forest that holds back the waters of the rainy season to bless the dry that follows after. The problems of the trees are also without number. There is the problem of the East — to save its forests where now they abound. There is the problem of the West —

to make forests abound where now they are unknown. A forest murderously ruined by the lumberman's axe is like a field of battle when the fighting is over — a sight to make humanity weep. Not so the forest that springs into life from the treeless plain. And so the mission of Arbor Day varies as the trees themselves. One blessed thing, however, is common to all the Arbor Days of the land we love, and that is the spirit to make the most of God's useful and beautiful trees.

———

ARBOR DAY ASPIRATION

BY JOHN RUSKIN

WE will try to make some small piece of ground beautiful, peaceful, and fruitful. We will have no untended or unthought-of creatures upon it. We will have flowers and vegetables in our gardens, plenty of corn and grass in our fields. We will have some music and poetry; the children shall learn to dance and sing it; perhaps some of the old people, in time, may also. We will have some art; and little by little some higher art and imagination may manifest themselves among us — nay — even perhaps an uncalculating and uncovetous wisdom, as of rude Magi, presenting gifts of gold and frankincense.

THE VIOLETS

BY AMANDA B. HARRIS

HAS any one, I wonder, ever classed and enumerated the blues of violets? I am sure it must have taken all the words that ever represent blue. They are turquoise, they are amethystine, they are sapphire, azure, cerulean. They are like the blue ether, like blue precious stones; like eyes of blue. They pale into lavender; they darken to purple. There are varieties in sky-blue with purple streaks; in deep violet striped with a lighter tint; in palest blue, with heavy shadings; and some that lack but little of being red.

THE DISCIPLINE OF GARDENING

BY JOHN WILLIAM COLE

THERE is such a close affinity between a proper cultivation of a flower-garden, and a right discipline of the mind, that it is almost impossible for any thoughtful person that has made any proficiency in the one, to avoid paying a due attention to the other. That industry and care which are so requisite to cleanse a garden from all sorts of weeds will naturally suggest to him how much more expedient it would be to exert the same diligence in eradicating all sorts of prejudices, follies, and vices from the

mind, where they will be as sure to prevail, without
a great deal of care and correction, as common weeds,
in a neglected piece of ground.

And as it requires more pains to extirpate some
weeds than others, according as they are more firmly
fixed, more numerous, or more naturalized to the
soil; so those faults will be found the most difficult
to be suppressed which have been of the longest
growth, and taken the deepest root; which are more
predominant in number, and most congenial to
the constitution.

FOR POSTERITY

BY ALEXANDER SMITH

A MAN does not plant a tree for himself, he plants
it for posterity. And, sitting idly in the sunshine, I
think at times of the unborn people who will, to
some small extent, be indebted to me. Remember
me kindly, ye future men and women!

ARBOR DAY

BY PROF. B. PICKMAN MANN, SON OF HORACE MANN
(*Extract from Letter*)

THE project of connecting the planting of trees
with the names of authors is a beautiful one, and one
certain to exert a beneficial influence upon the
children who participate in these exercises. The

institution of an "Arbor Day" is highly commendable from its artistic consequences, and cannot fail to result in great benefit to the climate and to the commercial interests of the country when it becomes an institution of general adoption.

PLANT TREES

BY J. WILSON

THE young should plant trees in recognition of the obligations they owe to those who planted trees for them. The old should plant trees to illustrate their hope for the future, and their concern for those who are to come after them. The economist should plant trees, especially in the prairie country, and beautify the landscape and ameliorate the sweep of the north wind. And as we plant trees on Arbor Day a kindred feeling to that experienced on the Fourth of July should possess us. For the time being we are one in mind; we are one people engaged in something to do good to mankind.

WASTE PLACES

BY GEN. SAMUEL F. CARY

(*Extract from Letter*)

IMPARTING to waste places more than their pristine beauty and associating the names of departed loved ones with our work is a poetic and sublime conception. It symbolizes our faith in a resurrection to a higher and better life when the hard struggles of this sin-cursed world are passed.

THE COMMONEST DELIGHT

BY CHARLES DUDLEY WARNER

To own a bit of ground, to scratch it with a hoe, to plant seeds and watch their renewal of life — this is the commonest delight of the race, the most satisfactory thing one can do.

ARBOR DAY

BY THOMAS B. STOCKWELL

The rapid approach of spring inevitably turns all thoughts to Arbor Day. That is naturally the *children's day* of all the year. After such a severe and stormy winter, with its snows and covering of ice, the buds bursting their bonds and the trees putting forth their leaves and flowers present an old, but this year an especially welcome, miracle.

In the years that have past we have learned some things that are possible for us, and as we face the new growth of nature at this time the question arises, to what use can we put any of our knowledge? First of all, we have been guided into the formal study of plant life as never before. The inherent power of all growing plants, even the smallest and humblest, has been brought to our notice and we have had our attention turned from books to plants, as equally the genuine sources of truth and inspiration. Now is the time in which we should profit by all this instruction in the past.

The countless lessons that may be learned from every plant that grows invite you all to a genuine feast of good things. I am sure that no longer is the study of plant or bird life in any of its marvelous forms accounted as foreign to the real work of the schoolroom, only it must have *results* and be based upon actual conditions. In such a way alone will it justify itself. Every school must be guided by *itself*, and in the same way each pupil must follow his own bent. There is no royal road by which all can penetrate to the secrets of Nature. She loves all who seek to know them, and she reveals the choicest and most wonderful to those who are most truly interested and who are inspired by the most genuine love for her.

The most difficult, and yet the most attractive, branch of nature study is that of birds, with their exquisite coloring which affords so much pleasure to the eye, their songs, so new and yet ever old, which ravish the ear, and yet elude the great majority of us. In no one respect does one's culture and training show itself as in the *real* study of bird life — not from books but from the object itself.

In these days of early spring what more engrossing pursuit can there be than to "rise with the lark" and make his acquaintance on the threshold of his own home! Quickness of perception and keenness of eyesight will soon be trained to an acuteness that seems almost foreign to the usual pupil at his ordinary school tasks. Even the teacher will find ample reward in the more intimate acquaintance with the feathered songsters of the open air through the wonderful acuteness of hearing and the marvelous power of location and identification which it gives her.

One practical object of our nature work will naturally be the beautification of our own school grounds. Why should we allow the place where we spend so much of our time, and what should be the happiest hours of the day, to be so barren and repulsive? To the adult it has ceased to possess any charms, because the outside world has become the field of his activity; hence, beyond supplying the necessities for the school life, he sees little use in all of the things that render the school attractive to the child.

The imagination of the child is now in full control and unless we give it rein within bounds, its education is dwarfed and misdirected to its permanent injury. In choice of a lot and in the adornment

of the grounds so much may be done to please the eye
or gratify the taste. Oftentimes what might appear
to parents, or even teachers and committees, as
blemishes, are transformed by childish imagination
to "things of beauty and a joy forever."

One way in which the taste of the child for self-
activity can be utilized and made to contribute
to the common notion of utility is by the cultivation
of the "school garden."

Fortunately we have not reached the point where
many of our school-houses have such contracted
grounds that they furnish no opportunity for such
a venture, and they are indeed few and far
between to whom such a possession would not
become a source of constant delight and of sub-
sequent profit.

In all our city and village schools the school garden
affords a field for the cultivation of a truer taste for
color, as well as a realistic sense of the useful and
practical.

Let this Arbor Day prove that past lessons in
shrubs and flowers, together with all information
relative to bird and insect life, have been sown on
good ground and are bearing fruit many fold. The
day may come sooner than we expect when the key
to solve many of the problems that beset us may be
furnished by some one, now a child, whose love for
this class of ideas will be surely traced to Arbor Day
and its celebration.

ARBOR DAY. ITS EDUCATING INFLUENCE

BY B. G. NORTHRUP

THE observance of Arbor Day has already led to the planting of myriads of trees in this country. Important as is this result, *the educating influence* of this work is of still higher value. One of these educating forces begins when children are thus led to plant not only trees, but tree-seeds, acorns, nuts, grape-stones or pits, and then to observe the wonderful miracles which the tree-life *they have started* is working out before them. What interest and profit, what growth of mind and heart they will gain as they watch the mysterious forces of these living germs, their marvelous assimilating power, carrying on a curious chemistry in their underground laboratory, linked with the mysterious apparatus of the leaves above, transforming coarse earth and even offensive filth into living forms of surpassing beauty and fragrance. It is something for a child who has dropped such a germ into the earth, to feel that he has made a lasting contribution to the natural beauty around him, for there is nothing more ennobling than the consciousness of doing something for future generations, which may prove a growing benefaction in coming years, a better monument than any in bronze or marble. The trees which children plant around the homestead and watch from seed to shoot, from bud to limb, and from flower to fruit, will be increasingly prized with a sentiment of companionship and almost of kinship as they grow into living memorials of happy youthful days. Thus, the educating influences of Arbor Day will manifest themselves more and more as the years go by, especially to all who apply Dr. Holmes's advice, and "make trees monuments of history and character," or appreciate his saying, "I have written many verses, but the best poems I have produced are the trees I have planted," or the striking words of Sir Walter Scott: "Planting and pruning trees I could work at from morning till night. There is a sort of self-congratulation, a little tickling self-flattery in the idea that while you are pleasing and amusing yourself, you are seriously contributing to the future welfare of the country."

As a result of Arbor Day, talks on trees and tree-planting are now common in our best schools. Every pupil should be led to observe, recognize, and admire our common trees, and thus come to realize that they form the finest drapery that adorns this earth in all lands. Such love of trees will tend to make them practical arborists. Let the parent as well as teacher, then, encourage every child — girl or boy — to plant, or help in planting, if too young to work alone, some flower, shrub, vine, or tree, to be known by his or her name. Such offspring they will watch with pride, as every month or year new beauties appear, and find peculiar pleasure in the parentage of trees, whether forest, fruit, or ornamental, a pleasure that never cloys, but grows with their growth. Such tree-planting is a grand discipline in foresight. Mental myopia means weakness and folly, while the habit of forecasting consequences is the condition of wisdom. Many youth will sow only where they can quickly reap. With them a meagre crop soon in hand outweighs a golden harvest long in maturing. The tree-planter can appreciate the apothegm, "To patiently work and wait, year after year, for the attainment of some far-off end, shows a touch of the sublime, and implies moral no less than mental heroism."

III

PRACTICAL SUGGESTIONS

PLANTING ON SCHOOL GROUNDS

BY CHARLES H. PECK

From *New York Arbor Day Annual*

AN IDEAL tree should be one with a sound, straight well-formed trunk, slightly tapering upward, free from branches to the full symmetrical head that it supports. This should be richly clothed with bright green, healthy foliage and bear at the proper time an abundance of beautiful, fragrant flowers, followed in due time by a crop of useful or edible fruit. Moreover, its wood should be valuable for economic purposes, and both it and the foliage should be free from the destructive and defiling attacks of parasitic insects and fungi. The tree should also be sufficiently hardy to endure without serious harm the frosts of winter and the droughts of summer. Probably no tree will satisfactorily meet all these requirements. Those that possess most of these qualities should be considered among the best for transplanting. The simplest standards by which any tree should be judged would be its hardiness, its attractiveness, and its usefulness. Any tree that lacks the first one of these qualities should be discarded. Possessing this character and either one of the others it is worthy of consideration. With this character and both the others it may be classed among the best for transplanting in school grounds.

Theoretically, trees may be transplanted late in autumn, after active growth has practically ceased, or early in spring before it has been renewed. The argument in favor of fall planting is that the rains of winter and early spring settle and compact the soil about the roots of the transplanted tree so that it is in excellent condition to begin growth as soon as the weather is favorable in spring. On the other hand, common practice sanctions the transplanting of trees in spring, and the designation of Arbor Day in spring presumes that this is at least a proper time for this work. Besides, it is possible so to do the work that it may not be necessary to wait for rain to settle the earth about the roots. It is very evident of course that a very young tree may be more easily and more successfully transplanted than an old one. A mere seedling scarcely a year old may be so carefully removed with the soil undisturbed about its roots and set in another place that it will scarcely suffer any check in its growth. But such seedlings are scarcely fit to be transplanted to school grounds. Unless specially protected they would soon be trodden down and destroyed. As a general rule it would probably be best to select trees two to four feet tall for transplanting. Such trees would not all be of the same age, for some trees make a much more rapid growth the first two or three years of life than others. Some of the evergreen cone-bearing trees grow slowly at first and then can not well endure the full light of the sun. It would be well that these should be a little older when transplanted than the others.

In considering how the transplanting is to be done we must remember that a tree is a thing of life, that it cannot be removed from its place of growth and set in another place without interfering, for a time, with the regular operation of its vital forces. For this reason the transplanting should be done at a season when the vital forces are least active, and care should be taken to avoid as much as possible all injury to the roots of the tree both in taking it up and in resetting it. The time between the two operations should be as short as possible and during the interval the roots should be entirely protected from both sun and wind by covering them with damp moss or dipping them in a thin mud made by mixing rich soil and water, and then wrapping them with a coarse damp cloth or canvas. If the removal and resetting can be done on a cloudy day so much the better. Not even the fine fibrous rootlets should be allowed to become dry. It would be well if the hole could be prepared in advance for the reception of the tree. Let it be broad enough to receive the roots without any bending or cramping. It may

better be too broad than too narrow and a little
deeper around the margin than in the centre. It
would be better, if deep enough, that it receive a layer
of rich garden soil or leaf mold three or four inches
thick on which the tree may stand. A pile of similar
soil should be ready as soon as the tree is put in
position to sift over its roots and pack down upon
and between them. Settle this soil still more about
the fibrous roots by giving it a copious sprinkling
with a watering pot. Finally fill the hole with soil
and cover the surface with a layer of manure to act
as a mulch and keep the soil moist about the roots.
Put no manure in the hole nor in contact with the
roots. Plant no tree so near the school-house that
in after years it will unduly shade the windows and
darken the schoolroom. Do not plant the trees too
close to each other. Give them an abundance of
room to form broad, well-shaped heads. Before
taking up the tree to be transplanted it is well to cut
away any slender, feeble, irregular or superfluous
branches in order to reduce the head to good shape
and to diminish the demand that would otherwise
be made upon the roots for support at a time when
they are not able to supply the usual amount of
moisture and nourishment. If the tree is an
evergreen with a leading shoot do not by
any means cut back or injure the leading shoot.
Cut out the feeble branches and the irregular
ones that may have grown between the nodes,

cutting them close to the trunk that the wound may quickly heal.

The following native trees and shrubs are among the best for transplanting in our school grounds: white pine, balsam fir, tamarack, basswood, tulip tree, sugar maple, silver maple, wild black cherry, chestnut, paper birch, cranberry tree, winterberry.

————

DRAPER'S "TEN COMMANDMENTS" ON TREE PLANTING

1. Do not allow roots to be exposed to the sun, drying winds, or frost.

2. Prune, with a sharp clean cut, any broken or injured roots.

3. Have the holes large enough to admit all the roots without cramping.

4. Plant in fine loam, enriched with thoroughly decomposed manure.

5. Do not allow any green unfermented manure to come in contact with roots.

6. Spread out the roots in their natural position and work fine loam among them, making it firm and compact.

7. Do not plant too deep. Let upper roots be set an inch lower than before.

8. Remove all broken branches, and cut back at least one-half of the previous year's growth of wood.

9. If the season lacks the usual rainfall, water thoroughly twice a week.

10. After-culture! Keep soil in a good degree of fertility. Mulching the trees in autumn with manure is beneficial.

TEN PRINCIPLES OF PRUNING*

BY JULIA E. ROGERS

1. Pruning the roots lessens the food supply, and so retards top growth.

2. Pruning the top invigorates the branches that remain, the root system being unchanged.

3. Removing terminal buds induces forking, thus thickening the branching system. It checks wood production, and encourages the production of fruit and flowers.

4. Unpruned trees tend to wood production.

5. Summer pruning reduces the struggle among leaves and twigs for light and produces stronger buds for spring.

6. Winter pruning removes superfluous buds, inducing greater health in those that are left to develop.

7. Dead wood should be taken out at any season and burned.

8. The best time to prune, generally speaking, is just before the growth starts in the spring.

*From "The Tree Book," Doubleday, Page & Co.

9.   Early winter pruning is undesirable because the healing of wounds must wait until spring.

10.   Yearly pruning is better than pruning at less frequent intervals.

————

HOW TO PLANT A TREE*

BY JULIA E. ROGERS

I.   Dig the hole wider and deeper than the tree requires.   If the tree just fits into the socket the tips of the roots will meet a hard wall which they are too delicate to penetrate, hold fast to, or feed in.

II.   Be sure that the surface soil is hoarded at one side when the hole is dug.   This soil is mellow and full of plant food.   The under soil is harder and more barren.   Some rich garden soil can well be brought over and used instead of the subsoil.

III.   Take up as large a root system as possible with the tree you dig.   The smaller the ball of earth, the greater the loss of feeding roots and the danger of starvation to the tree.

IV.   Trim all torn and broken roots with a sharp knife.   A ragged wound below or above the ground is slow and uncertain in healing.   A clean, slanting cut heals soonest and surest.

V.   Set the tree on a bed of mellow soil with all its roots spread naturally.

VI.   Let the level be the same as before.   The tree's

————

* From "The Tree Book," Doubleday, Page & Co.

roots must be planted, but not buried too deep to breathe. A stick laid across the hole at the ground level will indicate where the tree "collar" should be.

VII. Sift rich earth, free from clods, among the roots. Hold the tree erect and firm; lift it a little to make sure the spaces are well filled underneath. Pack it well down with your foot.

VIII. If in the growing season, pour in water and let it settle away. This establishes contact between root hairs and soil particles, and dissolves plant food for absorption. If the tree is dormant do not water it.

IX. Fill the hole with dirt. Tramp in well as filling goes on. Heap it somewhat to allow for settling. If subsoil is used, put it on last. Make the tree firm in its place.

X. Prune the top to a few main branches and shorten these. This applies to a sapling of a few years whose head you are able to form. Older trees should also be pruned to balance the loss of roots. Otherwise transpiration of water from the foliage would be so great as to overtax its roots, not yet established in the new place. Many trees die from this abuse. People cannot bear to cut back the handsome top, though a handsomer one is soon supplied by following this reasonable rule.

XI. Water the tree frequently as it first starts. A thorough soaking of all the roots, not a mere sprinkling of the surface soil, is needed. Continuous growth depends on moisture in the soil. Drainage will remove the surplus water.

XII. Keep the surface soil free from cakes or cracks. This prevents excessive evaporation. Do not stir the soil deep enough to disturb the roots. Keep out grass and weeds.

KINDS OF TREES TO PLANT

ADAPTED FROM EDMUND SPENSER

THE sailing Pine; the Cedar, proud and tall;
  The vine-prop Elm; the Poplar, never dry;
The builder Oak, sole king of forests all;
The Aspen, good for staves; the Cypress, funeral;
The Laurel, meed for mighty conquerors
  And poets sage; the Fir, that weepeth still;
The Willow, worn of hopeless paramours;
  The Yew, obedient to the bender's will;
The Birch, for shafts; the Sallow, for the mill;
The warlike Beech; the Ash, for nothing ill;
The fruitful Apple, and the Platane round;
The carver Holm; the Maple seldom inward sound.

THE BEST TREES AND VINES

BY DR. W. J. MILNE

TREES best adapted for successful culture are the elm, maple, linden, ash, birch, beech, dogwood, pines, spruces, some of the willows, some of the poplars, the tulip tree, horse-chestnut, catalpa, laburnum, and oak.

The *shrubs* which seem best adapted to ornamentation are the deutzia, hydrangea, spirea, weigela, privet, arbor vitæ, flowering cherry, flowering plum, and hawthorn.

Among our best and hardiest *vines* are the clematis, the bitter sweet, wistaria, trumpet vine, honeysuckle, morning glory, Virginia creeper, and ampelopsis veitchii.

The best plants for bedding purposes seem to be pansies, verbenas, geranium, coleuses, centaurea, and hybrid roses.

Beautiful beds may be formed by planting seeds of the portulaca, pansies, verbenas, zinnias, asters, dahlias, petunias, chrysanthemums, nasturtiums, balsams, phlox, sweet William, and seeds of other well-known plants.

SCHOOL ENVIRONMENT

From *Idaho Arbor Day Manual*

THE improvement and care of the school grounds by the pupils well illustrates the force of custom in creating an appreciation of the beautiful and in developing a disposition to respect public property. What is done by the organizer of the school in creating this public sentiment can, in a measure at least, be accomplished by any teacher or superintendent who really desires to beautify the school grounds under his care. Do we not as teachers greatly underestimate our influence in nurturing the sometimes almost extinguished æsthetic and nature loving instincts of our pupils? Do we fully realize how much it means to the coming citizen to early inculcate a high regard for public property — how much it means for character to create, even during the kindergarten years, the disposition so often expressed by both boys and girls when asked about some improvement on the school premises, "Oh! please may I help?"

THE SCHOOL GARDEN

BY L. C. CORBETT

A school garden should be considered as a laboratory in which the different steps in the life of a plant are to be illustrated. The nature of the soil, the importance of the fertilization, and the conditions essential to germination, as well as the conditions conducive to growth, can all be illustrated in a logical and impressive manner in the school garden. Field excursions may be the ideal way of conducting nature study work with reasoning minds, but with minds that are being trained to a logical system and in a consecutive and systematic fashion the school garden affords facilities not to be approached in field excursions. Field excursions offer disconnected fragments of the history of natural objects, while the school garden furnishes opportunities for observing plants from seed time to harvest.

A PLEA

BY HENRY VAN DYKE

Do NOT rob or mar a tree, unless you really need what it has to give you. Let it stand and grow in virgin majesty, ungirdled and unscarred, while the trunk becomes a firm pillar of the forest temple, and the branches spread abroad a refuge of bright green leaves for the birds of the air.

IMPROVEMENT OF SCHOOL GROUNDS

BY PROF. L. H. BAILEY

ONE'S training for the work of life is begun in the home and fostered in the school. This training is the result of a direct and conscious effort on the part of the parent and teacher, combined with the indirect result of the surroundings in which the child is placed. The surroundings are more potent than we think, and they are usually neglected. It is probable that the antipathy to farm life is often formed before the child is able to reason on the subject. An attractive playground will do more than a profitable wheat crop to keep the child on the farm.

Begin with the Fundamentals, not with the Details
—If an artist is to make a portrait, he first draws a few bold strokes, representing the general outline. He "blocks out" the picture. With the general plan well in mind, he gradually works in the incidentals and the details — the nose, eyes, beard.

Most persons reverse this natural order when they plant their grounds. They first ask about the kind of roses, the soil for snowballs, how far apart hollyhocks shall be planted. It is as if the artist first asked about the color of the eyes and the fashion of the necktie; or as if the architect first chose the color or paint and then planned his building. The result of this type of planting is that there is no plan, and the yard means nothing when it is done. Begin with the plan, not with the plants.

The Place should mean something — The home ground should be homelike, retired, and cozy. The school ground should be set off from the bare fields, and should be open enough to allow of playgrounds. It should be hollow — well planted on the side, open in the interior. The side next the highway should contain little planting. The place should be a picture, not a mere collection of trees and bushes.

Keep the Center of the Place Open — Do not scatter the trees over the place. They will be in the way. The boys will break them down. Moreover, they do not look well when scattered over the whole area. When an artist makes a picture with many people in it, he does not place the persons one by one all over his canvas; he masses them. Thereby he secures a stronger effect. He focuses attention rather than distributes it.

Next comes the planting. Let it be irregular and natural. First of all, cover up the outhouses. Then plant heavily on the side, or in the direction of the prevailing wind. Leave openings in your plan wherever there are views to be had of fine old trees, attractive farm homes, a brook, or a beautiful hill or field. Throw a handful of shrubs into the corners by the steps and about the bare corners of the building. Give room for the children to play, and make the place a picture at the same time. Three or four trees may be planted near the building to shade it, but the heaviest planting should be on the sides.

The Kinds of Plants for the Main Planting — One great principle will simplify the matter; the main planting should be for foliage effects. That is, think first of giving the place a heavy border mass. Flowers are mere decorations.

Select those trees and shrubs which are the commonest, because they are the cheapest, hardiest, and most likely to grow. There is no district so poor and bare that enough plants cannot be secured, without money, for the schoolyard. You will find them in the woods, in old yards, along fences. It is little matter if no one knows their names. What is handsomer than a tangled fence-row?

Scatter in a few trees along the fence and about the buildings. Maples, basswood, elms, ashes, buttonwood, pepperidge, oaks, beeches, birches, hickories, poplars, a few trees of pine or spruce or hemlock — any of these are excellent. If the country is bleak, a rather heavy planting of evergreens above the border, in the place of so much shrubbery, is excellent.

For shrubs, use the common things to be found in the woods and swales, together with roots which can be had in every old yard. Willows, osiers, witch-hazel, dogwood, wild roses, thorn apples, haws, elders, sumac, wild honeysuckles — these and others can be found in every school district. From the farmyards can be secured snowballs, spireas, lilacs, forsythias, mock-oranges, roses, snowberries, barberries, flowering currants, honeysuckles, and the like.

Vines can be used to excellent purpose on the outbuildings or on the school-house itself. The common wild Virginia creeper is the most serviceable.

Kinds of Plants for Decoration — Against these heavy borders and in the angles about the building many kinds of flowering plants can be grown. The flowers are much more easily cared for in such positions than they are in the middle of the lawn, and they also show off better. Hollyhocks are very effective.

More than one-third of all public schools will probably always be in the country. They will have most intimate relations with rural life. We must make that life attractive to the pupils. In Europe there are school gardens, and similar plans are recommended for this country. It is certainly desirable that some area be set aside for the actual cultivation of plants by the children, and for the grow ⁓ ing of specimens to be used in the schoolroom.

HINTS FOR THE FIRST SCHOOL GARDEN

BY EDITH GOODYEAR ALGER

From *School Gardens*

BEGIN early — early enough to stir up enthusiasm before it is time to stir up the soil; early enough to transplant all rubbish from the school grounds before it is time to plant seeds.

Have the children decide what the garden is to be, and here is a wide range; it may be a little ornamental "posy bed" cared for by all the children, a wild flower and fern garden of plants transplanted from woods and fields, a flower garden in which each child has a row, or a flower and vegetable garden divided into individual plots. The individual plot plan is undoubtedly to be preferred wherever practicable, and there are few village or rural schools where there is not room for the plot system. The individual garden arouses a personal responsibility and interest invaluable to the child. The plots should be small — good results can be obtained on a plot two feet square. Large plots which overtax the children to keep in perfect condition often prove so discouraging that they are neglected.

Having agreed upon the type of garden, the location should be determined. Lead the children to study carefully the conditions of sunshine and shadow, dryness and moisture, etc., and let them decide upon the best place for the garden, and *why*. The garden must not encroach upon the playground too much.

When these points are settled, decide how the space chosen for the garden is to be divided; the number, size, and position of the beds; number, size, and direction of the walks, etc. All actual measurements and calculations should be made by the children, and plans drawn to scale.

Breaking up and fertilizing the soil, raking, staking out beds and walks, must all be done systematically, with a reason for each process.

The older children should be supplied with notebooks in which to keep a written record of their work in the garden.

It is best to select for cultivation in the first school

garden a few varieties of very common vegetables, and hardy, easily grown flowers. Class-room study of the seeds and instruction regarding planting should be given before planting takes place. Some kinds of seeds may be given to the children to plant in boxes at home before it is time to plant out-of-doors, and the seedlings thus secured transplanted at the proper time.

Work in the school garden should be conducted in an orderly, intelligent manner — the children should always understand, not only what they are doing, but also just why it has to be done. Avoid planting so much land or so many kinds of seeds that care and careful study cannot be given to the garden and all it contains.

Remember that the best crop to be gathered from the school garden is the live interest in plant life, and the love of wholesome, useful out-of-door work gained by the children.

FOREST CULTURE

BY HORACE GREELEY

MONEY can be more profitably and safely invested in lands covered by young timber than anything else. The parent who would invest a few thousand for the benefit of his children or grandchildren, while young, may buy woodlands which will be worth twenty times their present cost within the next twenty years. But better even than this would it be to buy up rocky, craggy, naked hillsides, and eminences which have been pastured to death, and shutting out the cattle inflexibly, scratch these over with plow, mattock, hoe, or pick, as circumstances shall dictate; plant them thickly with chestnut, walnut, hickory, white oak, and the seeds of locust and white pine. Plant thickly and of divers kinds, so as to cover the ground promptly and choke out weeds and shrubs, with full purpose to thin and prune as circumstances shall dictate. Many farmers are averse to planting timber because they think nothing can be realized therefrom for the next twenty or thirty years, which is as long as they expect to live. But this is a grave miscalculation. Let us suppose a rocky, hilly pasture lot of ten or twenty acres, rudely scratched over as I have suggested, and thickly seeded with hickory nuts and white oak acorns only. Within five years it will yield abundantly of hoop-poles, though the better, more promising half be left to mature, as they should be; two years later another and larger crop of hoop-poles may be cut, still sparing the best, and thenceforth a valuable crop of timber may be taken from the land; for if cut at the proper season (October to March), at least two thrifty sprouts will start from every stump; and so that wood will yield a clear income each year, while the best trees are steadily growing and maturing. I do not advise restriction to those two species of timber, but I insist that a young plantation of forest trees may and should yield a clear income in every year after its fourth.

CRIMINAL TREATMENT OF TREES

ANONYMOUS

THE REV. MR. EGLESTON once called attention, in a forcible and sensible way, to the reckless and criminal treatment of our forests in general and of our good friends the trees in particular. His simple statement that nothing in nature except a man is more valuable than a tree, reminds one of the late Edward Jaffray's judgment that only killing a man was worse than cutting down a tree. The Laurel Hill Association seems likely to become foremost among societies for the prevention of cruelty to trees. The need of active measures to defend these preservers of our springs, these guardians of our rivers, these shelterers of our fields and gardens, from wanton outrage and careless, thriftless despoiling, is forcing itself on public attention, a cry of protest that gains force from the desolating fires among the Western pines, and the miserable pillage of our own Adironack preserves.

Arbor Day in the public schools is doing something toward the replenishing of treeless regions, restoring forest trees to their former habitation, and also toward the extermination of savagery toward all tree growth from the boys of this generation. Heredity from the slayers of trees in their fight with the primeval woods, will require heroic treatment. A boy with a hatchet is still a desolator, and with an axe he is a scourge second only to the forest burner; when he grows to manhood his greed is proof against all sentiment or suggestion of remoter consequences.

For centuries now the matchless forests of this country have been faced with the cry of "Kill! Kill!" There has been no mercy and no recourse. Slaughter has waged unhindered and unrebuked. Timber forests, with unlimited supply under care and culture, have been ruined. The waste has been more than the product. For bark, for charcoal and firewood, for fence posts and railroad ties, for lumber and shingles, for spars and ship-timbers, for woodenware, matches, and even toothpicks, the woods have been flayed alive. We have wasted our inheritance until the resulting shame is beginning to show. Forest laws that are sharp and usable as axes are demanded. The ownership of woodland must not carry the right to abuse it. Lands that are important water preserves should be protected the same as public reservoirs. Private ownership which has proved detrimental to public interests should be suppressed by public purchases. All possible restraints must be put on the marauders and incendiaries of the woods. For toleration of this criminal treatment of trees has reached its limit. The sentiment of our people is ready to sustain the hand of justice in the defense of these true friends of man.

And this correction of an evil will prove a change of heart in our people. The freedom and needs of our civilization have in this particular blunted our sensibilities. We have become callous to some serious affronts and wrongs. A whole village has been known to stand by, while a century-old tree, the pride and beauty of a street, has been killed to widen a road or to make room for some petty building. Such outrages have been perpetrated with a coolness that confessed to unconsciousness of wrong. The remedy for such things is education. Somebody must teach our people the rights and the dignity of a tree. They know its money value, but there is something more they need to know and to feel. There is a sanctity in natural growth which goes up to the sublimity of the great mountains. To violate this is to degrade ourselves. To despise or to degrade the splendid things about us is to prove ourselves unworthy of them. The Palisades of the Hudson can be made a signboard or a stone quarry, but the people who would so use them, or who would suffer such desecration of them, would sink as low in the scale of man as they would fall in the esteem of the world. This world is something more than a workshop. And a sin against the sanctity of any created thing is a sin against our own souls.

KNOW THE TREES

BY AUSTIN C. APGAR

ARBOR DAY, when in all the schools we are talking and singing about the beauties of nature in all her forms, and especially about the grandeur, the stateliness, and the usefulness of the trees, is a good time for us to resolve to know the different kinds of trees in our neighborhood. No one can appreciate much without knowing much. First, we must know trees by name, and, gradually, we will learn to know many interesting things about each in regard to the time when the buds burst in the spring, when the blossoms are to be found, when the fruit is ripe, when the leaves fall, all the changes in color of foliage that take place during the year, and many other characteristics. "The day we first know a tree by name will be the day when our interest and enjoyment in that tree will begin."

THE A B C OF LANDSCAPE GARDENING
Anonymous

(a) Keep lawn centers open.
(b) Plant in masses.
(c) Avoid straight lines.

Remove the rickety fences; tear down the dilapidated buildings and sheds; send the tin cans, broken boxes, and cinder piles the way of all useless things; clear the yards; in the place of the aforetime rubbish, grow things. This idea means good taste, at home as well as at school; neat lawns, whether the premises be large or small; clean roads; clean streets; clean alleys; the abatement of nuisances; the elevation of farm as well as of city life; the cultivation of interest in the moral, intellectual, and physical welfare of the community; and the creation of enthusiasm and love for the beautiful and the good.

DO

Make your street and yard in front and rear as clean and attractive as possible.

Destroy weeds.

Burn or bury rubbish.

Pick up loose paper.

Plant shrubs, vines, and flower seeds.

DON'T

Throw paper and fruit-skins on to the sidewalk, when baskets or boxes are near at hand.

Mark walls of buildings.

Injure shade trees or flower beds.

Spit on floors and sidewalks.

Throw stones at birds, for they destroy worms and insects and aid in making the town beautiful.

SUGGESTIONS FOR ARBOR DAY OBSERVANCE

BY ALFRED STONE

ARBOR DAY had its origin with a view to creating a community of interest and active coöperation in the work of annual tree-planting on a day set aside for that specific purpose, with a prearranged plan of where to plant them and what trees should be planted. In this way it was hoped that treeless streets and barren commons would be transformed and beautified, that unattractive towns would be made attractive, and waste places would be redeemed.

It is to be hoped that its original purpose may be revived and that the day may be again devoted to actual tree-planting in every hamlet, village, town, and city in the state.

Let the citizens get together in meetings of such societies as are already formed under whatever name they may be called — village improvement societies, men's clubs, women's clubs, boys' clubs, St. Andrew's societies, church clubs, it matters not which, but in some way get together — appoint committees and accomplish something worth while in the way of tree-planting.

At this meeting appoint at least six committees.

1. To select the place or places where the planting of trees is most demanded and where they will do the greatest good to the greatest number, and have stakes driven where each tree is to be planted.

2. To coöperate with committee number one, determine the number and kind of trees that are wanted, select and purchase them in ample season to be delivered and heeled in readiness for planting, and to distribute them on Arbor Day.

3. To raise the funds to pay for the trees, digging the holes, and procuring proper earth in which to plant them, assessing those whose estates are to be directly benefited in accordance with the benefit they will receive and their ability to pay, and collecting from the community at large enough to make up the deficit.

4. To arrange for digging the holes of the right size and depth, and procuring proper earth in which to plant the trees if the

soil where they are to be planted is not fit for the purpose. In many communities the holes would have to be dug and the piles of earth deposited near so that tree-planting alone should be the work for Arbor Day. In other communities, especially in farming communities, all of the work might be done on Arbor Day.

5. To procure a luncheon to be given in some grove, hall, school-house, church or vestry, and listen to the reports of the committees showing what had been done, and outlining a plan for next year's Arbor Day; to be followed by addresses, reading of poetry, music, and singing of songs appropriate to the occasion.

6. To arrange a programme for the after-dinner exercises, as indicated above. And it is recommended that the addresses be of a practical kind, on such subjects as: The benefits of arboriculture; What trees to plant in different locations according to soil, environment, wind and ocean exposure; How to prepare trees for transplanting, care of them in transportation, and how to plant them and care for them after planting.

IV

THE SEASON

PIPPA'S SONG

BY ROBERT BROWNING

From *Pippa Passes*

THE year's at the spring
And day's at the morn;
Morning's at seven;
The hillside's dew-pearled;
The lark's on the wing;
The snail's on the thorn;
God's in His heaven —
All's right with the world!

———

HOME THOUGHTS FROM ABROAD

BY ROBERT BROWNING

I

OH, TO be in England now that April's there!
And whoever wakes in England sees, some morning,
    unaware,
That the lowest boughs and the brushwood sheaf
Round the elm-tree bole are in tiny leaf,
While the chaffinch sings on the orchard bough
In England — now!

II

And after April, when May follows,
And the whitethroat builds, and all the swallows!
Hark, where my blossomed pear-tree in the hedge
Leans to the field and scatters on the clover
Blossoms and dewdrops — at the bent spray's
    edge —
That's the wise thrush; he sings each song twice
    over,
Lest you should think he never could recapture
The first fine careless rapture!
And though the fields look rough with hoary dew,
All will be gay when noontide wakes anew
The buttercups, the little children's dower
—Far brighter than this gaudy melon-flower!

———

THE WISTFUL DAYS*

BY ROBERT UNDERWOOD JOHNSON

WHAT is there wanting in the Spring?
    The air is soft as yesteryear;
    The happy-nested green is here,
And half the world is on the wing.
    The morning beckons, and like balm
    Are westward waters blue and calm.
Yet something's wanting in the Spring.

* By permission of the Century Co., New York.

What is it wanting in the Spring?
  O April, lover to us all,
  What is so poignant in thy thrall
When children's merry voices ring?
  What haunts us in the cooing dove
  More subtle than the speech of Love,
What nameless lack or loss of Spring?

Let Youth go dally with the Spring,
  Call her the dear, the fair, the young;
  And all her graces ever sung
Let him, once more rehearsing, sing.
  They know, who keep a broken tryst,
  Till something from the Spring be missed
We have not truly known the Spring.

SPRING

BY ALFRED TENNYSON

From *In Memoriam*

Now fades the last long streak of snow,
  Now burgeons every maze of quick
  About the flowering squares, and thick
By ashen roots the violets blow.

Now rings the woodland loud and long,
  The distance takes a lovelier hue,
  And drown'd in yonder living blue
The lark becomes a sightless song.

Now dance the lights on lawn and lea,
   The flocks are whiter down the vale,
   And milkier every milky sail
On winding stream or distant sea;

Where now the seamew pipes, or dives
   In yonder greening gleam, and fly
   The happy birds, that change their sky
To build and brood; that live their lives

From land to land; and in my breast
   Spring wakens too; and my regret
   Becomes an April violet,
And buds and blossoms like the rest.

FROM

GOD OF THE OPEN AIR *

BY HENRY VAN DYKE

WHILE the tremulous leafy haze on the woodland
   is spreading,
And the bloom on the meadow betrays where May
   has been treading;
While the birds on the branches above, and the
   brooks flowing under,
Are singing together of love in a world full of wonder,

* From " Music and Other Poems," copyright, 1904, by Charles
Scribner's Sons.

(Lo, in the marvel of Springtime, dreams are changed
    into truth!)
Quicken my heart, and restore the beautiful hopes of
    youth.

By the faith that the flowers show when they bloom
    unbidden,
By the calm of the river's flow to a goal that is
    hidden,
By the trust of the tree that clings to its deep founda-
    tion,
By the courage of wild birds' wings on the long
    migration,
(Wonderful secret of peace that abides in Nature's
    breast!)
Teach me how to confide, and live my life, and rest.

NEWS OF SPRING *

BY MAURICE MAETERLINCK

From *Old Fashioned Flowers*

I HAVE seen the manner in which Spring stores up
sunshine, leaves and flowers and makes ready, long
beforehand, to invade the North. Here, on the
ever balmy shores of the Mediterranean — that
motionless sea which looks as though it were under
glass — where, while the months are dark in the rest

* By special permission of M. Maeterlinck and Dodd, Mead
& Co.

of Europe, Spring has taken shelter from the wind and the snows in a palace of peace and light and love, it is interesting to detect its preparations for traveling in the fields of undying green. I can see clearly that it is afraid, that it hesitates once more to face the great frost-traps which February and March lay for it annually beyond the mountains. It waits, it dallies, it tries its strength before resuming the harsh and cruel way which the hypocrite winter seems to yield to it. It stops, sets out again, revisits a thousand times, like a child running round the garden of its holidays, the fragrant valleys, the tender hills which the frost has never brushed with its wings. It has nothing to do here, nothing to revive, since nothing has perished and nothing suffered, since all the flowers of every season bathe here in the blue air of an eternal summer. But it seeks pretexts, it lingers, it loiters, it goes to and fro like an unoccupied gardener. It pushes aside the branches, fondles with its breath the olive-tree that quivers with a silver smile, polishes the glossy grass, rouses the corollas that were not asleep, recalls the birds that had never fled, encourages the bees that were workers without ceasing; and then, seeing, like God, that all is well in the spotless Eden, it rests for a moment on the ledge of a terrace which the orange-tree crowns with regular flowers and with fruits of light, and, before leaving, casts a last look over its labor of joy and entrusts it to the sun.

SPRING*

BY RICHARD HOVEY

I SAID in my heart, "I am sick of four walls and a
    ceiling.
I have need of the sky.
I have business with the grass.
I will up and get me away where the hawk is
    wheeling,
Lone and high.
And the slow clouds go by.
I will get me away to the waters that glass
The clouds as they pass,
To the waters that lie
Like the heart of a maiden aware of a doom drawing
    nigh
And dumb for sorcery of impending joy.
I will get me away to the woods.
Spring, like a huntsman's boy,
Halloos along the hillsides and unhoods
The falcon in my will.
The dogwood calls me, and the sudden thrill
That breaks in apple blooms down country roads
Plucks me by the sleeve and nudges me away.
The sap is in the boles to-day,
And in my veins a pulse that yearns and goads."

* From "Along the Trail," copyright by Small, Maynard &
Co. Used by permission of the present publishers, Duffield & Co.

When I got to the woods, I found out
What the Spring was about,
With her gypsy ways
And her heart ablaze,
Coming up from the south
With the wander-lure of witch songs in her mouth.
For the sky
Stirred and grew soft and swimming as a lover's
    eye
As she went by;
The air
Made love to all it touched, as if its care
Were all to spare;
The earth
Prickled with lust of birth;
The woodland streams
Babbled the incoherence of the thousand dreams
Wherewith the warm sun teems.
And out of the frieze
Of the chestnut trees
I heard
The sky and the fields and the thicket find a voice
    in a bird.

   .   .   .   .

Spring in the world!
And all things are made new!
There was never a mote that whirled
In the nebular morn,
There was never a brook that purled

When the hills were born,
There was never a leaf uncurled —
Not the first that grew —
Nor a bee-flight hurled,
Nor a bird-note skirled,
Nor a cloud-wisp swirled
In the depth of the blue,
More alive and afresh and impromptu, more
thoughtless and certain and free.

. . . .

In the re-wrought sphere
Of the new-born year —
Now, now,
When the greenlet sings on the red-bud bough
Where the blossoms are whispering, "I and thou," —
"I and thou,"
And a lass at the turn looks after her lad with a dawn
on her brow,
And the world is just made — now!

Spring in the heart!
With her pinks and pearls and yellows!
Spring, fellows,
And we too feel the little green leaves a-start
Across the bare-twigged winter of the mart.
The campus is reborn in us to-day;
The old grip stirs our hearts with new-old joy;
Again bursts bonds for madcap holiday
The eternal boy.

For we have not come here for long debate
Nor taking counsel for our household order,
Howe'er we make a feint of serious things, —
For all the world as in affairs of state
A word goes out for war along the border
To further or defeat the loves of kings.
We put our house to rights from year to year;
But that is not the call that brings us here;
We have come here to be glad.

. . . .

A road runs east and a road runs west
From the table where we sing;
And the lure of the one is a roving quest;
And the lure of the other a lotus dream.
And the eastward road leads into the West
Of the lifelong chase of the vanishing gleam;
And the westward road leads into the East,
Where the spirit from striving is released,
Where the soul like a child in God's arms lies
And forgets the lure of the butterflies.
And west is east, if you follow the trail to the end;
And east is west, if you follow the trail to the end;
And the East and the West in the spring of the world
    shall blend.

As a man and a woman that plight
Their troth in the warm spring night.
And the spring for the East is the sap in the heart
    of a tree;

And the spring for the West is the will in the wings
    of a bird;
But the spring for the East and the West alike
    shall be
An urge in their bones and an ache in their spirit,
    a word
That shall knit them in one for Time's foison, once
    they have heard.

   .   .   .   .

So we are somehow sure,
By this dumb turmoil in the soul of man,
Of an impending something. When the stress
Climbs to fruition, we can only guess
What many-seeded harvest we shall scan;
But from one impulse, like a northering sun,
The innumerable outburst is begun,
And in that common sunlight all men know
A common ecstasy
And feel themselves at one.
The comradeship of joy and mystery
Thrills us more vitally as we arouse,
And we shall find our new day intimate
Beyond the guess of any long ago.
Doubting or elate,
With agony or triumph on our brows,
We shall not fail to be
Better comrades than before;
For no new sense puts forth in us but we
Enter our fellows' lives thereby the more.

And three great spirits with the spirit of man
Go forth to do his bidding.   One is free,
And one is shackled, and the third, unbound,
Halts yet a little with a broken chain
Of antique workmanship, not wholly loosed,
That dangles and impedes his forthright way.
Unfettered, swift, hawk-eyed, implacable,
The wonder-worker, Science, with his wand,
Subdues an alien world to man's desires.
And Art with wide imaginative wings
Stands by, alert for flight, to bear his lord
Into the strange heart of that alien world
Till he shall live in it as in himself
And know its longing as he knows his own.
Behind a little, where the shadows fall,
Lingers Religion with deep-brooding eyes,
Serene, impenetrable, transpicuous
As the all-clear and all-mysterious sky,
Biding her time to fuse into one act
Those other twain, man's right hand and his left.

For all the bonds shall be broken and rent in sunder,
And the soul of man go free
Forth with those three
Into the lands of wonder;
Like some undaunted youth,
Afield in quest of truth,
Rejoicing in the road he journeys on
As much as in the hope of journey done.

And the road runs east, and the road runs west,
That his vagrant feet explore;
And he knows no haste and he knows no rest,
And every mile has a stranger zest
Than the miles he trod before;
And his heart leaps high in the nascent year,
When he sees the purple buds appear:
For he knows, though the great black frost may blight
The hope of May in a single night,
That the spring, though it shrink back under the bark
But bides its time somewhere in the dark —
Though it comes not now to its blossoming,
By the thrill in his heart he knows the spring;
And the promise it makes perchance too soon,
It shall keep with its roses yet in June;
For the ages fret not over a day,
And the greater to-morrow is on its way.

APRIL*

BY JOHN BURROUGHS

From *A Year in the Fields*

IF WE represent the winter of our northern climate
by a rugged snow-clad mountain, and summer by
a broad fertile plain, then the intermediate belt,
the hilly and breezy uplands, will stand for spring,
with March reaching well up into the region of the

* By special permission of Houghton, Mifflin & Co.

snows, and April lapping well down upon the greening fields and unloosened currents, not beyond the
limits of winter's sallying storms, but well within
the vernal zone — within the reach of the warm
breath and subtle, quickening influences of the plain
below. At its best, April is the tenderest of tender
salads made crisp by ice or snow water. Its type
is the first spear of grass. The senses — sight,
hearing, smell — are as hungry for its delicate and
almost spiritual tokens as the cattle are for the first
bite of its fields. How it touches one and makes
him both glad and sad! The voices of the arriving
birds, the migrating fowls, the clouds of pigeons
sweeping across the sky or filling the woods, the elfin
horn of the first honey-bee venturing abroad in the
middle of the day, the clear piping of the little frogs
in the marshes at sundown, the camp-fire in the
sugar-bush, the smoke seen afar rising over the trees,
the tinge of green that comes so suddenly on the
sunny knolls and slopes, the full translucent streams,
the waxing and warming sun — how these things
and others like them are noted by the eager eye and
ear! April is my natal month, and I am born again
into new delight and new surprises at each return of
it. Its name has an indescribable charm to me.
Its two syllables are like the calls of the first birds —
like that of the phœbe-bird, or the meadow-lark.
Its very snows are fertilizing, and are called the poor
man's manure.

Then its odors! I am thrilled by its fresh and indescribable odors — the perfume of the bursting sod, of the quickened roots and rootlets, of the mold under the leaves, of the fresh furrows. No other month has odors like it. The west wind the other day came fraught with a perfume that was to the sense of smell what a wild and delicate strain of music is to the ear. It was almost transcendental. I walked across the hill with my nose in the air taking it in. It lasted for two days. I imagined it came from the willows of a distant swamp, whose catkins were affording the bees their first pollen; or did it come from much farther — from beyond the horizon, the accumulated breath of innumerable farms and budding forests? The main characteristic of these April odors is their uncloying freshness. They are not sweet, they are oftener bitter, they are penetrating and lyrical. I know well the odors of May and June, of the world of meadows and orchards bursting into bloom, but they are not so ineffable and immaterial and so stimulating to the sense as the incense of April.

The April of English literature corresponds nearly to our May. In Great Britain the swallow and the cuckoo usually arrive by the middle of April; with us their appearance is a week or two later. Our April, at its best, is a bright, laughing face under a hood of snow, like the English March, but presenting

sharper contrasts, a greater mixture of smiles and
tears and icy looks than are known to our ancestral
climate. Indeed, Winter sometimes retraces his
steps in this month, and unburdens himself of the
snows that the previous cold has kept back; but we
are always sure of a number of radiant, equable
days — days that go before the bud, when the sun
embraces the earth with fervor and determination.
How his beams pour into the woods till the mold
under the leaves is warm and emits an odor!
The waters glint and sparkle, the birds gather in
groups, and even those unwont to sing find a voice.
On the streets of the cities, what a flutter, what
bright looks and gay colors! I recall one pre-
eminent day of this kind last April. I made a note
of it in my notebook. The earth seemed suddenly
to emerge from a wilderness of clouds and chilliness
into one of these blue sunlit spaces. How the
voyagers rejoiced! Invalids came forth, old men
sauntered down the street, stocks went up, and the
political outlook brightened.

Such days bring out the last of the hibernating
animals. The woodchuck unrolls and creeps out
of his den to see if his clover has started yet. The
torpidity leaves the snakes and the turtles, and they
come forth and bask in the sun. There is nothing
so small, nothing so great, that it does not respond
to these celestial spring days, and give the pendulum
of life a fresh start.

April is also the month of the new furrow. As soon as the frost is gone and the ground settled, the plow is started upon the hill, and at each bout I see its brightened mold-board flash in the sun. Where the last remnants of the snowdrift lingered yesterday the plow breaks the sod to-day. Where the drift was deepest the grass is pressed flat, and there is a deposit of sand and earth blown from the fields to windward. Line upon line the turf is reversed, until there stands out of the neutral landscape a ruddy square visible for miles, or until the breasts of the broad hills glow like the breasts of the robins.

Then who would not have a garden in April? to rake together the rubbish and burn it up, to turn over the renewed soil, to scatter the rich compost, to plant the first seed or bury the first tuber! It is not the seed that is planted, any more than it is I that is planted; it is not the dry stalks and weeds that are burned up, any more than it is my gloom and regrets that are consumed. An April smoke makes a clean harvest.

I think April is the best month to be born in. One is just in time, so to speak, to catch the first train, which is made up in this month. My April chickens always turn out best. They get an early start; they have rugged constitutions. Late chickens cannot stand the heavy dews, or withstand the predaceous hawks. In April all nature starts with you. You have not come out your hibernaculum too early or too late; the time is ripe, and, if you do not keep pace with the rest, why, the fault is not in the season.

————

APRIL

BY HENRY WADSWORTH LONGFELLOW

WHEN the warm sun, that brings
   Seed-time and harvest, has returned again,
'Tis sweet to visit the still wood, where springs
   The first flower of the plain.

I love the season well,
   When forest glades are teeming with bright forms,
Nor dark and many-folded clouds foretell
   The coming-in of storms.

From the earth's loosened mold
   The sapling draws its sustenance, and thrives:
Though stricken to the heart with winter's cold,
   The drooping tree revives.

The softly warbled song
   Comes through the pleasant woods, and colored
     wings
Are glancing in the golden sun, along
   The forest openings.

And when bright sunset fills
   The silver woods with light, the green slope throws
Its shadow in the hollows of the hills,
   And wide the upland glows.

And when the day is gone,
  In the blue lake, the sky, o'erreaching far,
Is hollowed out, and the moon dips her horn,
  And twinkles many a star.

Inverted in the tide
  Stand the gray rocks, and trembling shadows
    throw,
And the fair trees look over, side by side,
  And see themselves below.

Sweet April, many a thought
  Is wedded unto thee, as hearts are wed;
Nor shall they fail, till, to its autumn brought,
  Life's golden fruit is shed.

————

THE COMING OF SPRING

BY HANS CHRISTIAN ANDERSEN

IT WAS far in January, and all day the snow was
pelting down, but toward evening it grew calm.
The sky looked as if it had been swept, and had
become more lofty and transparent. The stars
looked as if they were quite new, and some of them
were amazingly bright and pure. It froze so hard
that the snow creaked, and the upper rind of snow
might well have grown hard enough to bear the
sparrows in the morning dawn. These little birds
hopped up and down where the sweeping had

been done; but they found very little food, and were not a little cold.

"Piep!" said one of them to another; "they call this a new year, and it is worse than the last! We might just as well have kept the old one. I'm dissatisfied, and I've a right to be so."

"Yes; and the people ran about and fired off shots to celebrate the new year," said a little shivering sparrow; "and they threw pans and pots against the doors, and were quite boisterous with joy, because the old year was gone. I was glad of it too, because I hoped we should have had warm days; but that has come to nothing — it freezes much harder than before. People have made a mistake in reckoning the time!"

"That they have!" a third put in, who was old, and had a white poll; "they've something they call the calendar — it's an invention of their own — and everything is to be arranged according to that; but it won't do. When Spring comes, then the year begins, and I reckon according to that."

"But when will Spring come?" the others inquired.

"It will come when the stork comes back. But his movements are very uncertain, and here in towns no one knows anything about it; in the country they are better informed. Shall we fly out there and wait? There, at any rate, we shall be nearer to Spring."

And away they flew.

Out in the country it was hard Winter, the snow

creaked, and the sparrows hopped about in the ruts, and shivered. "Piep! when will Spring come? it is very long in coming!"

"Very long," sounded from the snow-covered hill, far over the field. It might be the echo which was heard; or perhaps the words were spoken by yonder wonderful old man, who sat in wind and weather high on a heap of snow.

"Who is that old man yonder?" asked the sparrows.

"I know who he is," quoth an old raven, who sat on the fence-rail. "It is Winter, the old man of last year. He is not dead, as the calendar says, but is guardian to little Prince Spring, who is to come. Yes, Winter bears sway here. Ugh! the cold makes you shiver, does it not, you little ones?"

"Yes. Did I not tell the truth?" said the smallest sparrow; "the calendar is only an invention of man, and is not arranged according to Nature! They ought to leave these things to us, who are born cleverer than they."

And one week passed away, and two passed away. The sunbeam glided along over the lake, and made it shine like burnished tin. The snowy covering on the field and on the hill did not glitter as it had done; but the white form, Winter himself, still sat there, his gaze fixed unswervingly upon the south. He did not notice that the snowy carpet seemed to sink as it were into the earth, and that here and there a little grass-green patch appeared, and that all these patches were crowded with sparrows.

"Kee-wit! kee-wit! Is Spring coming now?"

"Spring!" The cry resounded over field and meadow, and through the black-brown woods, where the moss still glimmered in bright green upon the tree trunks, and from the south the first two storks came flying through the air.

"WHEN THE GREEN GITS BACK IN THE TREES"*

BY JAMES WHITCOMB RILEY

IN THE spring when the green gits back in the trees,
    And the sun comes out and stays,
And your boots pull on with a good tight squeeze,
    And you think of your barefoot days;
When you ort to work and you want to not,
    And you and yer wife agrees
It's time to spade up the garden lot —
    When the green gits back on the trees —
    Well, work is the least of my idees
    When the green, you know, gits back in the trees.

When the green gits back in the trees, and bees.
    Is a buzzin' aroun' agin,
In that kind of a lazy "go-as-you please"
    Old gait they hum roun' in;

---

*By permission of the publishers, Bobbs-Merrill Co.

When the ground's all bald where the hayrick stood,
  And the crick's riz, and the breeze
Coaxes the bloom in the old dogwood,
  And the green gits back in the trees —
  I like, as I say, in sich scenes as these,
  The time when the green gits back in the trees.

When the whole tail-feathers o' winter-time
  Is all pulled out and gone,
And the sap it thaws and begins to climb,
  And the sweat it starts out on
A feller's forrerd, a-gittin' down
  At the old spring on his knees —
I kind o' like jes' a-loaferin' roun',
  When the green gits back in the trees —
  Jes' a-potterin' roun' as I — durn — please —
  When the green, you know, gits back in the trees.

THE FIRST OF APRIL

BY MORTIMER COLLINS

Now, if to be an April fool
  Is to delight in the song of the thrush,
To long for the swallow in air's blue hollow,
  And the nightingale's riotous music-gush,
And to painted vision of cities Elysian
  Out away in the sunset-flush —
Then I grasp my flagon and swear thereby,
We are April fools, my love and I.

And if to be an April fool
  Is to feel contempt for iron and gold,
For the shallow fame at which most men aim —
  And to turn from worldlings cruel and cold
To God in His splendor, loving and tender,
  And to bask in His presence manifold —
Then by all the stars in His infinite sky,
We are April fools, my Love and I.

———

SONG: A MAY MORNING
BY JOHN MILTON

Now the bright morning star, Day's harbinger,
Comes dancing from the East, and leads with her
The flowery May, who from her green lap throws
The yellow cowslip and the pale primrose.
Hail, bounteous May, that doth inspire
Mirth, and youth, and warm desire;
Woods and groves are of thy dressing,
Hill and dale doth boast thy blessing.
Thus we salute thee with our early song.
And welcome thee, and wish thee long.

———

SPRING MAGIC
BY CHARLES DICKENS

WHAT man is there over whose mind a bright
spring morning does not exercise a magic influence?

Carrying him back to the days of his childish sports, and conjuring up before him the old green field with its gently waving trees, where the birds sang as he has never heard them since, where the butterfly fluttered far more gaily than he ever sees him now in all his ramblings, where the sky seemed bluer, and the sun shone more brightly, where the air blew more freshly over greener grass and sweeter-smelling flowers, where everything wore a richer and more brilliant hue than it is ever dressed in now!   Such are the deep feelings of childhood, and such are the impressions which every lovely object stamps upon its heart!

WHY YE BLOSSOME COMETH BEFORE YE LEAFE*

BY OLIVER HERFORD

ONCE Hoary Winter chanced — alas!
Alas! hys waye mistaking —
A leafless apple-tree to pass
Where Spring lay dreaming.   "Fie, ye lass!
Ye lass had best be waking,"
Quoth he, and shook hys robe, and, lo!
Lo! forth didde flye a cloud of snowe.

----

*From " The Bashful Earthquake and other Fables," copyright 1898, by Oliver Herford; published by Charles Scribner's Sons.

Now in ye bough an elfe there dwelte,
An elfe of wondrous powere,
That when ye chillye snowe didde pelte,
With magic charm each flake didde melte,
Didde melte into a flowere;
And Spring didde wake and marvelle how,
How blossomed so ye leafless bough.

———

SPRING

(After Meleager)

BY ANDREW LANG

Now the bright crocus flames, and now
 The slim narcissus takes the rain,
And, straying o'er the mountain's brow,
 The daffodillies bud again.
The thousand blossoms wax and wane
 On wold, and heath, and fragrant bough,
 But fairer than the flowers art thou,
Than any growth of hill or plain.

Ye gardens, cast your leafy crown,
That my Love's feet may tread it down,
Like lillies on the lilies set;
 My love, whose lips are softer far
 Than drowsy poppy petals are,
And sweeter than the violet.

THE RETURN OF SPRING*

BY HENRY WADSWORTH LONGFELLOW

From *Charles D'Orléans*

Now Time throws off his cloak again
Of ermined frost, and wind, and rain,
And clothes him in the embroidery
Of glittering sun and clear blue sky.
With beast and bird the forest rings,
Each in his jargon cries or sings;
And Time throws off his cloak again
Of ermined frost, and wind, and rain.

River, and fount, and tinkling brook
Wear in their dainty livery
Drops of silver jewelry;
In new-made suit they merry look;
And Time throws off his cloak again
Of ermined frost, and wind, and rain.

THE MONTH OF APPLE BLOSSOMS

BY HENRY WARD BEECHER

It MAKES no difference that you have seen forty
or fifty springs, each one is as new, every process
as fresh, and the charm as fascinating as if you had

* By permission of the publishers, Houghton, Mifflin & Co.

never witnessed a single one. Nature works the same things without seeming repetition. There, for instance, is the apple-tree. Every year since our boyhood it has been doing the same thing; standing low to the ground, with a round and homely head, without an element of grandeur or poetry, except once a year. In the month of May, apple-trees go a-courting. Love is evermore father of poetry. And the month of May finds the orchard no longer a plain, sober business affair, but the gayest and most radiant frolicker of the year. We have seen human creatures whose ordinary life was dutiful and prosaic; but when some extraordinary excitement of grief, or, more likely, of deep love, had thoroughly mastered them, they broke forth into a richness of feeling, an inspiration of sentiment, that mounted up into the very kingdom of beauty, and for the transient hour they glowed with the very elements of poetry. And so to us seems the apple-tree. From June to May it is a homely, duty-performing, sober, matter-of-fact tree. But May seems to stir up a love-beat in its veins.

The old round-topped, crooked-trunked, and ungainly boughed fellow drops all world-ways and takes to itself a new idea of life. Those little stubbed spurs, that all the year had seemed like rheumatic fingers, or thumbs and fingers, stiffened and stubbed by work, now are transformed. Forth they put a little head of buds, which a few rains and days of encouraging warmth solicit to a cluster of blossoms. At first rosy and pink, then opening purely white. And now, where is your old, homely tree?

All its crookedness is hidden by the sheets of blossoms. The whole top is changed to a royal dome. The literal, fruit-bearing tree is transfigured, and glows with raiment whiter and purer than any white linen. It is a marvel and a glory! What if you have seen it before, ten thousand times over? An apple-tree in full blossom is like a message, sent fresh from heaven to earth, of purity and beauty. We walk around it reverently and admiringly. We are never tired of looking at its profusion. Homely as it ordinarily is, yet now it speaks of the munificence of God better than any other tree.

The very glory of God seems resting upon it! It is a little inverted hemisphere, like that above it, and it daily mimics with bud and bloom the stars that nightly blossom out into the darkness above it. Though its hour of glory is short, into it is concentrated a magnificence which puts all the more stately trees into the background. If men will not admire, insects and birds will!

There, on the very topmost twig, that rises and falls with willowy motion, sits that ridiculous but

sweet-singing bobolink, singing, as a Roman-candle
fizzes, showers of sparkling notes. If you stand at
noon under the tree, you are in a very beehive.
The tree is musical. The blossoms seem, for a
wonder, to have a voice. The odor is not a rank
atmosphere of sweet. Like the cups from which
it is poured, it is delicate and sweet. You feel
as if there were a timidity in it, that asked
your sympathy, and yielded to solicitation. You
do not take it whether you will or not, but,
though it is abundant, you follow it rather
than find it. Is not this gentle reserve, that yields
to real admiration, but hovers aloof from coarse
or cold indifference, a beautiful trait in woman or
apple-tree?

But was there ever such a spring? Did orchards
ever before praise God with such choral colors?
The whole landscape is aglow with orchard radiance.
The hillsides, the valleys, the fields, are full of
blossoming trees. The pear and cherry have shed
their blossoms. The ground is white as snow with
their flakes. Let other trees boast their superiority
in other months. But in the month of May, the very
flower-month of the year, the crown and glory of all
is the apple-tree.

Therefore, in my calendar, hereafter, I do ordain
that the name of this month be changed. Instead
of May, let it henceforth be called in my kingdom,
"The Month of the Apple Blossoms."

AN ANGLER'S WISH*

BY HENRY VAN DYKE

WHEN tulips bloom in Union Square,
And timid breaths of vernal air
  Go wandering down the dusty town,
Like children lost in Vanity Fair;

When every long, unlovely row
Of westward houses stands aglow,
  And leads the eyes towards sunset skies
Beyond the hills where green trees grow —

Then weary seems the street parade,
And weary books, and weary trade:
  I'm only wishing to go a-fishing;
For this the month of May was made.

II

I guess the pussy-willows now
Are creeping out on every bough
  Along the brook; and robins look
For early worms behind the plow.

The thistle-birds have changed their dun
For yellow coats, to match the sun;
  And in the same array of flame
The dandelion show's begun.

---

*From " The Builders and other Poems," copyright 1897, by
Charles Scribner's Sons.

The flocks of young anemones
Are dancing round the budding trees:
    Who can help wishing to go a-fishing
In days as full of joy as these?

III

I think the meadow-lark's clear sound
Leaks upward slowly from the ground,
    While on the wing the blue-birds ring
Their wedding-bells to woods around.

The flirting chewink calls his dear
Behind the bush; and very near,
    Where water flows, where green grass grows,
Song-sparrows gently sing, "Good cheer."

And, best of all, through twilight's calm,
The hermit-thrush repeats his psalm.
    How much I'm wishing to go a-fishing
In days so sweet with music's balm!

IV

'Tis not a proud desire of mine;
I ask for nothing superfine;
    No heavy weight, no salmon great,
To break the record — or my line:

Only an idle little stream,
Whose amber waters softly gleam,
    Where I may wade, through woodland shade,
And cast the fly, and loaf, and dream:

Only a trout or two, to dart
From foaming pools and try my art:
   No more I'm wishing — old-fashioned fishing,
And just a day on Nature's heart.

———

APRIL*

BY LLOYD MIFFLIN

AMONG the maple-buds we heard the tones
   Of April's earliest bees, although the days
   Seemed ruled by Mars. The veil of gathering haze
Spread round the silent hills in bluest zones.
Deep in the pines the breezes stirred the cones,
   As on we strolled within the wooded ways,
   There where the brook, transilient, softly plays
With muffled plectrum on her harp of stones;
Onward we pushed amid the yielding green
   And light rebounding of the cedar boughs,
Until we heard — the forest lanes along,
   Above the lingering drift of latest snows —
The thrush outpour, from coverts still unseen,
   His rare ebulliency of liquid song!

———

MRS. JUNE'S PROSPECTUS

BY SUSAN COOLIDGE

MRS. JUNE is ready for school,
   Presents her kind regard,

* By permission of the author.

And for all her measures and rule
   Refers to the following

CARD

To parents and friends: Mrs June,
   Of the firm of Summer and Sun,
Announces the opening of her school,
   Established in the year one.

An unlimited number received;
   There is nothing at all to pay;
All that is asked is a merry heart,
   And time enough to be gay.

The Junior class will bring,
   In lieu of all supplies,
Eight little fingers and two little thumbs
   For the making of pretty sand-pies.

The Senior class, a mouth
   For strawberries and cream,
A nose apiece for a rose apiece,
   And a tendency to dream.

The lectures are thus arranged:
   Professor Cherry Tree
Will lecture to the Climbing Class,
   Terms of instruction — free.

Professor De-Forest Spring,
   Will take the class on Drink;

And the class in Titillation,
  Sage Mr. Bobolink.

Young Mr. Ox-Eye Daisy
  Will demonstrate each day
On Botany, on native plants,
  And the properties of hay.

Miss Nature, the class in Fun
  (A charming class to teach);
And the Swinging class and the Bird-nest class
  Miss Hickory and Miss Beech.

And the Sleepy class at night,
  And the Dinner class at noon,
And the Fat and Laugh and Roses class,
  They fall to Mrs. June.

And she hopes her little friends
  Will be punctual as the sun;
For the term, alas! is very short,
  And she wants them every one.

———

SPRING

BY DONALD G. MITCHELL (IK MARVEL)

From *Dream Life*

THE budding and blooming of spring seem to belong properly to the opening of the months. It is the season of the quickest expansion, of the warmest blood, of the readiest growth; it is the boy-age of the year. The birds sing in chorus in the spring — just as children prattle; the brooks run full — like the overflow of young hearts; the showers drop easily — as young tears flow; and the whole sky is as capricious as the mind of a boy.

Between tears and smiles, the year like the child struggles into the warmth of life. The old year, say what the chronologists will, lingers upon the very lap of spring, and is only fairly gone, when the blossoms of April have strewn their pall of glory upon his tomb, and the bluebirds have chanted his requiem.

It always seems to me as if an access of life came with the melting of the winter's snows; and as if every rootlet of grass that lifted its first green blade from the matted débris of the old year's decay bore my spirit upon it, nearer to the largess of Heaven.

A TOUCH OF NATURE*

BY THOMAS BAILEY ALDRICH

WHEN first the crocus thrusts its point of gold
Up through the still snow-drifted garden mold,
And folded green things in dim woods unclose
Their crinkled spears, a sudden tremor goes
Into my veins and makes me kith and kin

*By permission of the publishers, Houghton, Mifflin & Co.

To every wild-born thing that thrills and blows.
Sitting beside this crumbling sea-coal fire,
Here in the city's ceaseless roar and din,
Far from the brambly paths I used to know,
Far from the rustling brooks that slip and shine
Where the Neponset alders take their glow,
I share the tremulous sense of bud and brier,
And inarticulate ardors of the vine.

A SPRING RELISH*

BY JOHN BURROUGHS

From *Signs and Seasons*

THERE is a brief period in our spring when I like
more than at any other time to drive along the country roads, or even to be shot along by steam and have
the landscape presented to me like a map. It is at
that period, usually late in April, when we behold the
first quickening of the earth. The waters have sub-
sided, the roads have become dry, the sunshine has
grown strong and its warmth has penetrated the
sod; there is a stir of preparation about the farm and
all through the country. One does not care to see
things very closely; his interest in nature is not special, but general. The earth is coming to life again.
All the genial and more fertile places in the landscape are brought out; the earth is quickened in

* By permission of the publishers, Houghton, Mifflin & Co.

spots and streaks; you can see at a glance where man and nature have dealt the most kindly with it. The warm, moist places, the places that have had the wash of some building or of the road, or been subjected to some special mellowing influence, how quickly the turf awakens there and shows the tender green! See what the landscape would be, how much earlier spring would come to it, if every square yard of it was alike moist and fertile. As the later snows lay in patches here and there, so now the earliest verdure is irregularly spread over the landscape and is especially marked on certain slopes, as if it had blown over from the other side and lodged there.

A little earlier the homesteads looked cold and naked; the old farmhouse was bleak and unattractive; now Nature seems especially to smile upon it; her genial influences crowd up around it; the turf awakens all about as if in the spirit of friendliness. See the old barn on the meadow slope; the green seems to have oozed out from it and to have flowed slowly down the hill; at a little distance it is lost in the sere stubble. One can see where every spring lies buried about the fields; its influence is felt at the surface and the turf is early quickened there. Where the cattle have loved to lie and ruminate in the warm summer twilight, there the April sunshine loves to linger too, till the sod thrills to new life.

The home, the domestic feeling in nature is brought out and enhanced at this time; what man has done tells, especially what he has done well. Our interest centers in the farmhouses and in the influence that seems to radiate from there. The older the home, the more genial nature looks about it. The new architectural place of the rich citizen, with the barns and outbuildings concealed or disguised as much as possible — spring is in no hurry about it; the sweat of long years of honest labor has not yet fattened the soil it stands upon.

The full charm of this April landscape is not brought out till the afternoon. It seems to need the slanting rays of the evening sun to give it the right mellowness and tenderness, or the right perspective. It is, perhaps, a little too bald in the strong, white light of the earlier part of the day, but when the faint, four o'clock shadows begin to come out and we look through the green vistas, and along the farm lanes toward the west, or out across long stretches of fields above which spring seems fairly hovering, just ready to alight, and note the teams slowly plowing, the brightened moldboard gleaming in the sun now and then — it is at such times we feel its fresh, delicate attraction the most. There is no foliage on the trees yet; only here and there the red bloom of the soft maple, illuminated by the declining sun, shows vividly against the tender green of a slope beyond, or a willow, like a thin veil, stands out against a leafless wood. Here and there a little meadow watercourse is golden with marsh marigolds, or some fence border, or rocky streak of neglected pasture land, is thickly starred with the white flowers of the bloodroot. The eye can devour a succession of landscapes at such a time; there is nothing that sates or entirely fills it, but every spring token stimulates it and makes it more on the alert.

THE GLADNESS OF NATURE

BY WILLIAM CULLEN BRYANT

Is THIS a time to be cloudy and sad,
    When our mother Nature laughs around;
When even the deep blue heavens look glad,
    And gladness breathes from the blossoming
        ground?
There are notes of joy from the hang-bird and wren,
    And the gossip of swallows through all the sky;
The ground-squirrel gaily chirps by his den,
    And the wilding bee hums merrily by.

The clouds are at play in the azure space,
    And their shadows at play on the bright-green vale,
And here they stretch to the frolic chase,
    And there they roll on the easy gale.

There's a dance of leaves in that aspen bower,
    There's a titter of winds in that beechen tree,
There's a smile on the fruit, and a smile on the flower,
    And a laugh from the brook that runs to the sea.

And look at the broad-faced sun, how he smiles
  On the dewy earth that smiles in his ray
On the leaping waters and gay young isles;
  Ay, look, and he'll smile thy gloom away.

THE RETURN OF SPRING

BY BAYARD TAYLOR

A SPIRIT of beauty walks the hills,
  A spirit of love the plain;
The shadows are bright, and the sunshine fills
  The air with a diamond rain!

Before my vision the glories swim,
  To the dance of a tune unheard:
Is an angel singing where woods are dim,
  Or is it an amorous bird?

Is it a spike of azure flowers,
  Deep in the meadows seen,
Or is it the peacock's neck that towers
  Out of the spangled green?

Is a white dove glancing across the blue,
  Or an opal taking wing?
For my soul is dazzled through and through,
  With the splendor of the Spring.

A SPRING SONG

ANONYMOUS

OLD Mother Earth woke up from her sleep,
   And found she was cold and bare;
The winter was over, the spring was near,
   And she had not a dress to wear.
"Alas!" she sighed, with great dismay,
   "Oh, where shall I get my clothes?
There's not a place to buy a suit,
   And a dressmaker no one knows."

"I'll make you a dress," said the springing grass,
   Just looking above the ground,
"A dress of green of the loveliest sheen,
   To cover you all around."
"And we," said the dandelions gay,
   "Will dot it with yellow bright."
"I'll make it a fringe," said forget-me-not,
   "Of blue, very soft and light."

"We'll embroider the front," said the violets,
   "With a lovely purple hue."
"And we," said the roses, "will make you a crown
   Of red, jeweled over with dew."
"And we'll be your gems," said a voice from the
      shade,
   Where the ladies' ear-drops live —
"Orange is the color for any queen
   And the best we have to give."

Old Mother Earth was thankful and glad,
    As she put on her dress so gay;
And that is the reason, my little ones,
    She is looking so lovely to-day.

SPRING IN THE SOUTH*

BY HENRY VAN DYKE

Now in the oak the sap of life is welling,
    Tho' to the bough the rusty leafage clings;
Now on the elm the misty buds are swelling,
    See how the pine-wood grows alive with wings;
Blue-jays fluttering, yodeling and crying,
    Meadow-larks sailing low above the faded grass,
Red-birds whistling clear, silent robins flying —
    Who has waked the birds up?   What has come
      to pass?

Last year's cotton-plants, desolately bowing,
    Tremble in the March-wind, ragged and forlorn;
Red are the hillsides of the early plowing,
    Gray are the lowlands, waiting for the corn.
Earth seems asleep still, but she's only feigning;
    Deep in her bosom thrills a sweet unrest.
Look where the jasmine lavishly is raining
    Jove's golden shower into Danaë's breast!

---

* From "Music and other Poems," copyright, 1904, by Charles
Scribner's Sons.

Now on the plum the snowy bloom is sifted,
  Now on the peach the glory of the rose,
Over the hills a tender haze is drifted,
  Full to the brim the yellow river flows.
Dark cypress boughs with vivid jewels glisten,
  Greener than emeralds shining in the sun.
Who has wrought the magic? Listen, sweetheart,
    listen!
  The mocking-bird is singing Spring has begun.

Hark, in his song no tremor of misgiving!
  All of his heart he pours into his lay —
"Love, love, love, and pure delight of living:
  Winter is forgotten: here's a happy day!"
Fair in your face I read the flowery presage,
  Snowy on your brow and rosy on your mouth:
Sweet in your voice I hear the season's message —
  Love, love, love, and Spring in the South!

———

THE SPRING

BY JAMES SPEED

HAVE you ever gone into the woods on an early day,
a day when the wind was still cold, but in the south?
One of those days when the smile of the sun and the
soft noise of the wind make you know in some vague
way that spring is coming? If you have not, try it.
Go sit at the base of some old man of the woods
whose sides are gray and green with clinging lichens

and mosses and whose head shows the fight with winter storms and heavy sleets. Put your head against
his side, there is no sound; drop your head to the
ground, and yet no sound; but you know that he, too,
has heard the summons to awake; that spring is coming. Somehow you feel as you see the tender green
veiling the lightest twigs that the trees are vitally alive.

As the birds have their songs to tell of their love,
so the trees and the plants put forth their joy at the
marriage time by their odors which float everywhere
and make the spring air a thing to be remembered.
Have you ever been through the woods when the
wild grape vines were a mass of bloom? Was not
their odor as suggestive in a subtle way as the song
of the birds? So think of the trees, as people who
live in a little different world, but still part of the
throbbing life which is manifest everywhere.

––––––

AN INVITATION TO THE COUNTRY

BY WILLIAM CULLEN BRYANT

ALREADY, close by our summer dwelling,
  The Easter sparrow repeats her song;
A merry warbler, she chides the blossoms —
  The idle blossoms that sleep so long.

The bluebird chants, from the elm's long branches,
  A hymn to welcome the budding year.
The south wind wanders from field to forest,
  And softly whispers, "The spring is here."

Come, daughter mine, from the gloomy city,
   Before those lays from the elm have ceased:
The violet breathes, by our door, as sweetly
   As in the air of her native east.

Though many a flower in the wood is waking,
   The daffodil is our doorside queen;
She pushes upward the sward already,
   To spot with sunshine the early green.

No lays so joyous as these are warbled
   From wiry prison in maiden's bower;
No pampered bloom of the greenhouse chamber
   Has half the charm of the lawn's first flower.

Yet these sweet sounds of the early season,
   And these fair sights of its sunny days,
Are only sweet when we fondly listen,
   And only fair when we fondly gaze.

A VIOLIN MOOD

BY ROBERT HAVEN SCHAUFFLER

To-day the sense of spring fills all my frame,
   And, thrilling, stirs and throbs in me as when
The sap began to course like liquid flame
   In March in my old tree-home far from men.
   And now my voice grows warm and rich again
And full of vibrant, vernal murmuring,
   Re-echoing bird-notes out of brake and fen

That tell of youth and young love on the wing
And all the thousand joyous mysteries of Spring.

SPRING*

BY HENRY WADSWORTH LONGFELLOW

IN ALL climates spring is beautiful. The birds begin to sing; they utter a few joyful notes, and then wait for an answer in the silent woods. Those green-coated musicians, the frogs, make holiday in the neighboring marshes. They, too, belong to the orchestra of nature, whose vast theater is again opened, though the doors have been so long bolted with icicles, and the scenery hung with snow and frost like cobwebs. This is the prelude which announces the opening of the scene. Already the grass shoots forth, the waters leap with thrilling force through the veins of the earth, the sap through the veins of the plants and trees, and the blood through the veins of man. What a thrill of delight in springtime! What a joy in being and moving! Men are at work in gardens, and in the air there is an odor of the fresh earth. The leaf-buds begin to swell and blush. The white blossoms of the cherry hang upon the boughs like snowflakes; and ere long our next-door neighbor will be completely hidden from us by the dense green foliage. The

* By permission of the publishers, Houghton, Mifflin & Co.

Mayflowers open their soft blue eyes. Children are let loose in the fields and gardens. They hold buttercups under each other's chins, to see if they love butter. And the little girls adorn themselves with chains and curls of dandelions; pull out the yellow leaves to see if the schoolboy loves them, and blow the down from the leafless stalk, to find out if their mothers want them at home. And at night so cloudless and so still! Not a voice of living thing — not a whisper of leaf or waving bough — not a breath of wind — not a sound upon the earth or in the air! And overhead bends the blue sky, dewy and soft, and radiant with innumerable stars like the inverted bell of some blue flower, sprinkled with golden dust, and breathing fragrance. Or, if the heavens are overcast, it is no wild storm of wind and rain, but clouds that melt and fall in showers. One does not wish to sleep, but lies awake to hear the pleasant sound of the dropping rain.

APRIL DAYS

BY ALFRED TENNYSON

From *In Memoriam*

Dip down upon the northern shore,
   O sweet new year delaying long;
   Thou doest expectant nature wrong;
Delaying long, delay no more.

What stays thee from the clouded noons,
   Thy sweetness from its proper place?
   Can trouble live with April days,
Or sadness in the summer moons?

Bring orchis, bring the foxglove spire,
   The little speedwell's darling blue,
   Deep tulips dash'd with fiery dew;
Laburnums, dropping wells of fire.

O thou, new year, delaying long,
   Delayest the sorrow in my blood,
   That longs to burst a frozen bud,
And flood a fresher throat with song.

———

LINES WRITTEN IN EARLY SPRING

BY WILLIAM WORDSWORTH

I HEARD a thousand blended notes,
   While in a grove I sate reclined,
In that sweet mood when pleasant thoughts
   Bring sad thoughts to the mind.

To her fair works did Nature link
   The human soul that through me ran;
And much it grieved my heart to think
   What man has made of man.

Through primrose tufts, in that sweet bower,
   The periwinkle trailed its wreaths;

And 'tis my faith that every flower
 Enjoys the air it breathes.

The birds around me hopped and played;
 Their thoughts I cannot measure —
But the least motion which they made,
 It seemed a thrill of pleasure.

The budding twigs spread out their fan,
 To catch the breezy air;
And I must think, do all I can,
 That there was pleasure there.

If this belief from heaven be sent,
 If such be Nature's holy plan,
Have I not reason to lament
 What man has made of man?

V
TREES

THE MARSHES OF GLYNN*

BY SIDNEY LANIER

GLOOMS of the live-oaks, beautiful-braided and woven
With intricate shades of the vines that myriad-cloven
Clamber the forks of the multiform boughs —
      Emerald twilights —
      Virginal shy lights,
Wrought of the leaves to allure to the whisper of vows,
When lovers pace timidly down through the green
    colonnades
Of the dim sweet woods, of the dear dark woods,
Of the heavenly woods and glades,
That run to the radiant marginal sand-beach within
    The wide sea-marshes of Glynn; —

Beautiful glooms, soft dusks in the noonday fire —
Wildwood privacies, closets of lone desire,
Chamber from Chamber `parted with wavering
    arras of leaves —
Cells for the passionate pleasure of prayer to the
    soul that grieves,
Pure with a sense of the passing of saints through the
    wood,

* From "The Poems of Sidney Lanier." Copyright 1884, 1891,
by Mary D. Lanier; published by Charles Scribner's Sons.

Cool for the dutiful weighing of ill with good;
O braided dusks of the oak and woven shades of the
    vine,
While the riotous noonday sun of the June-day
    long did shine
Ye held me fast in your heart and I held you fast in
    mine;
But now when the noon is no more, and riot
    is rest,
And the sun is a-wait at the ponderous gate of the
    West,
And the slant yellow beam down the wood-aisle
    doth seem
Like a lane into heaven that leads from a dream,
Ay, now, when my soul all day hath drunken the
    soul of the oak,
And my heart is at ease from men, and the weari-
    some sound of the stroke
Of the scythe of time and the trowel of trade is low,
And belief overmasters doubt, and I know that I
    know,
And my spirit is grown to a lordly great compass
    within,
That the length and the breadth and the sweep of
    the Marshes of Glynn
Will work me no fear like the fear they have wrought
    me of yore
When length was fatigue, and when breadth was but
    bitterness sore,

And when terror and shrinking and dreary, unnam-
able pain
Drew over me out of the merciless miles of the plain,

Oh, now, unafraid, I am fain to face
The vast sweet visage of space.
To the edge of the wood I am drawn, I am drawn,
Where the gray beach glimmering runs, as a belt
of the dawn,

For a mete and a mark
To the forest dark:
So:

Affable live-oak, leaning low,
Thus — with your favor — soft, with a reverent hand
(Not lightly touching your person, lord of the
land!)
Bending your beauty aside, with a step I stand
On the firm-packed sand,

Free

By a world of marsh that borders a world of sea.

*   *   *   *   *   *   *   *   *

TALKS ON TREES*

BY OLIVER WENDELL HOLMES

From *The Autocrat of the Breakfast Table*

Don't you want to hear me talk trees a little now?
That is one of my specialties.

---

* By permission of Houghton, Mifflin & Co.

I want you to understand, in the first place, that I have a most intense, passionate fondness for trees in general, and have had several romantic attachments to certain trees in particular.

I shall speak of trees as we see them, love them, adore them in the fields, where they are alive, holding their green sunshades over our heads, talking to us with their hundred thousand whispering tongues, looking down on us with that sweet meekness which belongs to huge, but limited, organisms — which one sees in the brown eyes of oxen, but most in the patient posture, the outstretched arms, and the heavy-drooping robes of these vast beings endowed with life, but not with soul — which outgrow us and outlive us, but stand helpless — poor things! — while Nature dresses and undresses them, like so many full-sized, but under-witted, children.

Just think of applying the Linnæan system to an elm! Who cares how many stamens or pistils that little brown flower, which comes out before the leaf, may have to classify it by? What we want is the meaning, the character, the expression of a tree, as a kind and as an individual.

There is a mother-idea in each particular kind of tree, which, if well marked, is probably embodied in the poetry of every language. Take the oak, for instance, and we find it always standing as a type of strength and endurance. I wonder if you ever thought of the single mark of supremacy which distinguishes this tree from those around it? The others shirk the work of resisting gravity; the oak defies it. It chooses the horizontal direction for its limbs so that their whole weight may tell, and then stretches them out fifty or sixty feet, so that the strain may be mighty enough to be worth resisting. You will find, that, in passing from the extreme downward droop of the branches of the weeping willow to the extreme upward inclination of those of the poplar, they sweep nearly half a circle. At 90 degrees the oak stops short; to slant upward another degree would mark infirmity of purpose; to bend downwards, weakness of organization. The American elm betrays something of both; yet sometimes, as we shall see, puts on a certain resemblance to its sturdier neighbor.

It won't do to be exclusive in our taste about trees. There is hardly one of them which has not peculiar beauties in some fitting place for it. I remember a tall poplar of monumental proportions and aspect, a vast pillar of glossy green, placed on the summit of a lofty hill, and a beacon to all the country round. A native of that region saw fit to build his house very near it, and, having a fancy that it might blow down some time or other, and exterminate himself and any incidental relatives who might be "stopping" or "tarrying" with him — also laboring under the delusion that human life is under all circumstances to be preferred to vegetable existence — had the great poplar cut down. It is so easy to say, "It is only a poplar," and so much harder to replace its living cone than to build a granite obelisk!

I always tremble for a celebrated tree when I approach it for the first time. Provincialism has no scale of excellence in man or vegetable; it never knows a first-rate article of either kind when it has it, and is constantly taking second and third rate ones for Nature's best. I have often fancied the tree was afraid of me, and that a sort of shiver came over it as over a betrothed maiden when she first stands before the unknown to whom she has been plighted. Before the measuring tape the proudest tree of them all quails and shrinks into itself. All those stories of four or five men stretching their arms around it and not touching each other's fingers, of one's pacing the shadow at noon and making it so many hundred feet, die upon its leafy lips in the presence of the awful ribbon which has strangled so many false pretensions.

The largest actual girth I have ever found at five feet from the ground is in the great elm lying a stone's throw or two north of the main road (if my points of compass are right) in Springfield. But this has much the appearance of having been formed by the union of two trunks growing side by side.

The West Springfield elm and one upon Northampton meadows belong also to the first class of trees.

There is a noble old wreck of an elm at Hatfield, which used to spread its claws out over a circumference of thirty-five feet or more before they covered the foot of its bole up with earth. This is the American elm most like an oak of any I have ever seen.

What makes a first-class elm? Why, size, in the first place, and chiefly. Anything over twenty feet of clear girth, five feet above the ground and with a spread of branches a hundred feet across, may claim that title, according to my scale. All of them, with the questionable exception of the Springfield tree above referred to, stop, so far as my experience goes, at about twenty-two or twenty-three feet of girth and a hundred and twenty of spread.

Elms of the second class, generally ranging from fourteen to eighteen feet, are comparatively common. The queen of them all is that glorious tree near one of the churches in Springfield. Beautiful and stately she is beyond all praise. The "great tree" on Boston common comes in the second rank, as does the one at Cohasset, which used to have, and probably has still, a head as round as an apple-tree, and that at Newburyport, with scores of others which might be mentioned. These last two have, perhaps, been over-celebrated. Both, however, are pleasing vegetables. The poor old Pittsfield elm lives on its past reputation. A wig of false leaves is indispensable to make it presentable.

Go out with me into that walk which we call the Mall, and look at the English and American elms. The American elm is tall, graceful, slender-sprayed, and drooping as if from languor. The English elm is compact, robust, holds its branches up, and carries its leaves for weeks longer than our own native tree. Is this typical of the creative force on the two sides of the ocean, or not? Nothing but a careful comparison through the whole realm of life can answer this question.

There is a parallelism without identifying in the animal and vegetable life of the two continents, which favors the task of comparison in an extraordinary manner. Just as we have two trees alike in many ways, yet not the same, both elms, yet easily distinguishable, just so we have a complete flora and a fauna, which, parting from the same ideal, embody it with various modifications.

I have something more to say about trees. I have brought down this slice of hemlock to show you. Tree blew down in my woods (that were) in 1852. Twelve feet and a half round, fair girth; nine feet, where I got my section, higher up. This is a wedge, going to the centre, of the general shape of a slice of apple pie in a large and not opulent family. Length, about eighteen inches.

I have studied the growth of this tree by its rings, and it is curious. Three hundred and forty-two rings. Started, therefore, about 1510. The thickness of the rings tells of the rate at which it grew. For five or six years the rate was slow, then rapid for twenty years. A little before the year 1550 it began to grow very slowly, and so continued for about seventy years. In 1620 it took a new start and grew fast until 1714, then for the most part slowly until 1786, when it started again and grew pretty well and uniformly until within the last dozen years, when it seems to have got on sluggishly.

Look here. Here are some human lives laid down against the periods of its growth, to which they corresponded. This is Shakespeare's. The tree was seven inches in diameter when he was born; ten inches when he died. A little less than ten inches when Milton was born; seventeen when he died. Then comes a long interval, and this thread marks out Johnson's life, during which the tree increased from twenty-two to twenty-nine inches in diameter. Here is the span of Napoleon's career; the tree doesn't seem to have minded it.

I never saw the man yet who was not startled at looking on this section. I have seen many wooden preachers — never one like this. How much more striking would be the calendar counted on the rings of one of those awful trees which were standing when Christ was on earth, and where that brief mortal life is chronicled with the stolid apathy of vegetable being, which remembers all human history as a thing of yesterday in its own dateless existence!

INSCRIPTION FOR THE ENTRANCE TO A WOOD

BY WILLIAM CULLEN BRYANT

STRANGER, if thou hast learned a truth which needs
No school of long experience, that the world
Is full of guilt and misery, and hast seen
Enough of all its sorrows, crimes, and cares,
To tire thee of it, enter this wild wood
And view the haunts of Nature. The calm shade
Shall bring a kindred calm, and the sweet breeze
That makes the green leaves dance, shall waft a balm
To thy sick heart. Thou wilt find nothing here
Of all that pained thee in the haunts of men,
And made thee loathe thy life. The primal curse
Fell, it is true, upon the unsinning earth,
But not in vengeance. God hath yoked to guilt
Her pale tormentor, misery. Hence, these shades
Are still the abodes of gladness; the thick roof
Of green and stirring branches is alive
And musical with birds, that sing and sport

In wantonness of spirit; while below
The squirrel, with raised paws and form erect,
Chirps merrily. Throngs of insects in the shade
Try their thin wings and dance in the warm beam
That waked them into life. Even the green trees
Partake the deep contentment; as they bend
To the soft winds, the sun from the blue sky
Looks in and sheds a blessing on the scene.
Scarce less the cleft-born wild-flower seems to enjoy
Existence, than the winged plunderer
That sucks its sweets. The mossy rocks themselves,
And the old and ponderous trunks of prostrate trees
That lead from knoll to knoll a causey rude,
Or bridge the sunken brook, and their dark roots,
With all their earth upon them, twisting high,
Breathe fixed tranquillity. The rivulet
Sends forth glad sounds, and tripping o'er its bed
Of pebbly sands, or leaping down the rocks,
Seems, with continuous laughter, to rejoice
In its own being. Softly tread the marge,
Lest from her midway perch thou scare the wren
That dips her bill in water.* The cool wind,
That stirs the stream in play, shall come to thee,
Like one that loves thee nor will let thee pass
Ungreeted, and shall give its light embrace.

---

* The poem, as first published in the *North American Review*
for September, 1817, under the title "A Fragment," ended at
this point. The last lines were added in the first edition of the
Poems, in 1821.

THE APPEAL OF THE TREES

BY J. HORACE McFARLAND

From *Getting Acquainted with the Trees*

A TREE is never without interest to those whose eyes have been opened to some of the wonders and perfections of Nature. Nevertheless, there is a time in the year's round when each tree makes its special appeal. It may be in the winter, when every twig is outlined sharply against the cold sky, and the snow reflects light into the innermost crevices of its structure, that the elm is most admirable. When the dogwood has on its white robe in May and June, it then sings its song of the year. The laden apple-tree has a pure glory of the blossoms, and another warmer, riper glory of the burden of fruit, but we think most kindly of its flowering time.

Some trees maintain such a continuous show of interest and beauty that it is difficult to say on any day, "*Now* is this tulip or this oak at its very finest!"

A BALLAD OF TREES AND THE MASTER*

BY SIDNEY LANIER

INTO the woods my Master went,
Clean forspent, forspent.

* From "The Poems of Sidney Lanier," copyright 1884, 1891, by Mary D. Lanier, published by Charles Scribner's Sons.

Into the woods my Master came,
Forspent with love and shame.
But the olives they were not blind to Him;
The little gray leaves were kind to Him;
The thorn-tree had a mind to Him
When into the woods He came.

Out of the woods my Master went,
And He was well content.
Out of the woods my Master came,
Content with death and shame.
When Death and Shame would woo Him last,
From under the trees they drew Him last:
'Twas on a tree they slew Him — last,
When out of the woods He came.

WOODNOTES*

II

BY RALPH WALDO EMERSON

As the sunbeams stream through liberal space
And nothing jostle or displace,
So waved the pine-tree through my thought
And fanned the dreams it never brought.

* By permission of the publishers, Houghton, Mifflin & Co.
The stately white pine of New England was Emerson's favorite tree. . . . This poem records the actual fact; nearly every day, summer or winter, when at home, he went to listen to its song. The pine grove by Walden, still standing, though injured by time and fire, was one of his most valued possessions. He questioned whether he should not name his book "Forest Essays," for, he said, "I have scarce a day-dream

"Whether is better, the gift or the donor?
Come to me,"
Quoth the pine-tree,
"I am the giver of honor.
My garden is the cloven rock,
And my manure the snow;
And drifting sand-heaps feed my stock,
In summer's scorching glow.
He is great who can live by me:
The rough and bearded forester
Is better than the lord;
God fills the scrip and canister,
Sin piles the loaded board.
The lord is the peasant that was,
The peasant the lord that shall be;
The lord is hay, the peasant grass,
One dry, and one the living tree.
Who liveth by the ragged pine
Foundeth a heroic line;
Who liveth in the palace hall
Waneth fast and spendeth all.*

---

on which the breath of the pines has not blown and their shadow
waved." The great pine on the ridge over Sleepy Hollow was
chosen by him as his monument. When a youth, in Newton, he
had written, "Here sit Mother and I under the pine-trees, still
almost as we shall lie by and by under them."—(E. W. Emerson,
in the Centenary Edition.)

    * Compare the essay on "Manners": "The city would have died
out, rotted, and exploded, long ago, but that it was reinforced
from the fields. It is only country which came to town day
before yesterday that is city and court to-day."

He goes to my savage haunts,
With his chariot and his care;
My twilight realm he disenchants,
And finds his prison there.

"What prizes the town and the tower?
Only what the pine-tree yields;
Sinew that subdued the fields;
The wild-eyed boy, who in the woods
Chants his hymn to hills and floods,
Whom the city's poisoning spleen
Made not pale, or fat, or lean;
Whom the rain and the wind purgeth,
Whom the dawn and the day-star urgeth,
In whose cheek the rose-leaf blusheth,
In whose feet the lion rusheth.
Iron arms and iron mold,
That know not fear, fatigue or cold.
I give my rafters to his boat,
My billets to his boiler's throat,
And I will swim the ancient sea
To float my child to victory,
And grant to dwellers with the pine
Dominion o'er the palm and vine.
Who leaves the pine-tree leaves his friend,
Unnerves his strength, invites his end.
Cut a bough from my parent stem,
And dip it in thy porcelain vase;
A little while each russet gem

Will swell and rise with wonted grace;
But when it seeks enlarged supplies,
The orphan of the forest dies.
Whoso walks in solitude
And inhabiteth the wood,
Choosing light, wave, rock and bird,
Before the money-loving herd,
Into that forester shall pass,
From these companions, power and grace.
Clean shall he be, without, within,
From the old adhering sin,
All ill dissolving in the light
Of his triumphant piercing sight:
Not vain, nor sour, nor frivolous;
Not mad, athirst, nor garrulous;
Grave, chaste, contented, though retired,
And of all other men desired.
On him the light of star and moon
Shall fall with purer radiance down;
All constellations of the sky
Shed their virtue through his eye.
Him nature giveth for defense
His formidable innocence;
The mountain sap, the shells, the sea,
All spheres, all stones, his helpers be;
He shall meet the speeding year,
Without wailing, without fear;
He shall be happy in his love,
Like to like shall joyful prove;

He shall be happy whilst he woos,
Muse-born, a daughter of the Muse.

———

PINE NEEDLES

BY WILLIAM H. HAYNE

IF Mother Nature patches
    The leaves of trees and vines,
I'm sure she does her darning
    With the needles of the pines.

They are so long and slender;
    And sometimes, in full view,
They have their thread of cobwebs,
    And thimbles made of dew.

———

A TEMPLE

BY ANNA BAGSTAD

DID many of us ever really see a tree? We focus
our eyes on a great many things which in reality we
never see at all. How blind we are to the common
things around us — wilfully blind because they are
common! But it is the common things, after all,
that are the most wonderful.

Take one of the thousands and millions of leaves
on a tree. What is a leaf? It may not be so hard
to find a fairly satisfactory dictionary definition for

one; but with that and a little sense-perception, our knowledge ends. Any one who could tell us just what a leaf is, and how by some strange action of air and earth and sunlight it comes to be a leaf — his would transcend the wisdom of the ages.

Trees are common. Yes, but how long did it take Mother Nature, working incessantly, to form out of the low, one-celled plant, cruder and simpler than any grass or weed we know, the beautiful, noble monarch of the plant kingdom which we call a tree?

"The groves were God's first temples." And each tree is a temple for birds and bees. Its living columns are overlaid with the ruby and topaz of summer sunlight and with the pearl and diamond dust of winter. It is a shrine where the spirit of man may look up. It is a monument to what has been, a heavenward pointing testimony to the Power that lies at the heart of things.

———

TREES*

BY JULIA ROGERS

THE meaning of trees in a landscape — the beauty value of them — is oftenest overlooked by those who have always seen them. When crossing such

---

*From " The Tree Book," Doubleday, Page & Co.

a monotonous stretch of treeless country as the plains of Arizona that wait for irrigation, the Easterner for the first time has a full appreciation of the beauty of his familiar wooded hillsides and tree-lined streets. Out of the homesickness for forest scenery, as well as the necessity for protection and wood supply, came the great tree-planting crusade that swept over the Middle West and will yet dot every state with homes surrounded by groves.

THE REAL TREE

BY OLIVER WENDELL HOLMES

From *Over the Teacups*

WHAT a strange underground life is that which is lead by the organisms we call *trees!* These great fluttering masses of leaves, stems, boughs, trunks, are not the real tree. *They* live underground, and what we see are nothing more nor less than their *tails*.

Yes, a tree is an underground creature, with its tail in the air. All its intelligence is in its roots. All the senses it has are in its roots. Think what sagacity it shows in its search after food and drink! Somehow or other, the rootlets, which are its tentacles, find out there is a brook at a moderate distance from the trunk of the tree, and they make for it with all their might. They find every crack in

the rocks where there are a few grains of the nour-
ishing substance they care for, and insinuate themselves into its deepest recesses. When spring and
summer come, they let their tails grow, and delight
in whisking them about in the wind or letting them
be whisked about by it; for these tails are poor
passive things, with very little will of their own,
and bend in whatever direction the wind chooses
to make them. The leaves make a deal of noise
whispering. I have sometimes thought I could
understand them, as they talk with each other, and
that they seemed to think they made the wind as
they wagged forward and back. Remember what
I say. The next time you see a tree waving in the
wind recollect that it is the tail of a great underground, many-armed, polypus-like creature, which
is as proud of its caudal appendage, especially in
the summer time, as a peacock of his gorgeous
expanse of plumage.

Do you think there is anything so very odd about
that idea? Once get it well into your head and you
well find it renders the landscape wonderfully
interesting. There are as many kinds of tree-
tails as there are of tails to dogs and other quad-
rupeds. Study them as Dady Gilpin studied
them in his "Forest Scenery," but don't forget
that they are only the appendage of the underground vegetable polypus, the true organism to
which they belong.

A SPRAY OF PINE*

BY JOHN BURROUGHS

From *Signs and Seasons*

THE pine is the tree of silence. Who was the Goddess of Silence? Look for her altars amid the pines — silence above, silence below. Pass from deciduous woods into pine woods of a windy day, and you think the day has suddenly become calm. Then how silent to the foot! One walks over a carpet of pine needles almost as noiselessly as over the carpets of our dwellings. Do these halls lead to the chambers of the great that all noise should be banished from them? Let the designers come here and get the true pattern for a carpet — a soft yellowish brown, with only a red leaf, or a bit of gray moss, or a dusky lichen scattered here and there; a background that does not weary or bewilder the eye, or insult the ground-loving foot.

How friendly the pine-tree is to man — so docile and available as timber, and so warm and protective as shelter. Its balsam is salve to his wounds, its fragrance is long life to his nostrils; an abiding, perennial tree, tempering the climate, cool as murmuring waters in summer and like a wrapping of fur in winter.

---

* By permission of the publishers, Houghton, Mifflin & Co.

O DREAMY, GLOOMY, FRIENDLY TREES

BY HERBERT TRENCH

O DREAMY, gloomy, friendly Trees,
    I came along your narrow track
To bring my gifts unto your knees,
    And gifts did you give back;
For when I brought this heart that burns —
    These thoughts that bitterly repine —
And laid them here among the ferns
    And the hum of boughs divine,
Ye, vastest breathers of the air,
    Shook down with slow and mighty poise
Your coolness on the human care,
    Your wonder on its toys,
Your greenness on the heart's despair,
    Your darkness on its noise.

THE TWIG THAT BECAME A TREE

ANONYMOUS

THE tree of which I am about to tell you was once
a little twig. There were many others like it, and
the farmer came to look at them every day, to see
if they were all doing well.

By and by he began to take away the older and

stronger twigs, and one day he dug up this little tree and carried it away to an open field.

There its roots were again put into the soft, warm ground, and it held its pretty head up as if looking into the blue sky. Just at sunset the farmer's wife came out to look at the new tree.

"I wonder if I shall ever see apples growing on these twigs," she said.

The little tree heard it, and said softly: "We shall see! Come, gentle rain and warm sun, and let me be the first to give a fine, red apple to the farmer's wife."

And the rain and the sun did come, and the branches grew, and the roots dug deep into the soft ground, and at last, one bright spring day, the farmer's wife cried:

"Just see! One of our little trees has some blossoms on it! I believe that, small as it is, it will give me an apple this autumn."

But the farmer laughed and said: "Oh, it is not old enough to bear apples yet."

The little tree said nothing, but all to itself it thought: "The good woman shall have an apple this very year."

And she did. When the cool days of autumn came, and the leaves began to fade and grow yellow, two red apples hung upon one of the branches of the tree.

THE AGE OF TREES

ANONYMOUS

MAN counts his life by years; the oak, by centuries. At one hundred years of age the tree is but a sapling; at five hundred it is mature and strong; at six hundred the giant king of the greenwood begins to feel the touch of time; but the decline is as slow as the growth was, and the sturdy old tree rears its proud head and reckons centuries of old age just as it reckoned centuries of youth.

It has been said that the patriarchs of the forest laugh at history. Is it not true? Perhaps, when the balmy zephyrs stir the trees, the leaves whisper strange stories to one another. The oaks and the pines, and their brethren of the wood, have seen so many suns rise and set, so many seasons come and go, and so many generations pass into silence, that we may well wonder what "the story of the trees" would be to us if they had tongues to tell it, or we ears fine enough to understand.

THE PINE TREE

BY JOHN RUSKIN

From *Modern Painters*

THE tremendous unity of the pine absorbs and moulds the life of a race. The pine shadows rest

upon a nation. The northern peoples, century
after century, lived under one or other of the two
great powers of the pine and the sea, both infinite.
They dwelt amidst the forests as they wandered on
the waves, and saw no end nor any other horizon.
Still the dark, green trees, or the dark, green waters,
jagged the dawn with their fringe or their foam.
And whatever elements of imagination, or of warrior
strength, or of domestic justice, were brought down
by the Norwegian or the Goth against the dissolute-
ness or degradation of the south of Europe, were
taught them under the green roofs and wild pene-
tralia of the pine.

THE TREE*

BY JONES VERY

I LOVE thee when thy swelling buds appear
   And one by one their tender leaves unfold,
As if they knew that warmer suns were near,
   Nor longer sought to hide from winter's cold:
And when with darker growth thy leaves are seen,
   To veil from view the early robin's nest,
I love to lie beneath thy waving screen
   With limbs by summer's heat and toil oppressed;
And when the autumn winds have stripped thee bare,
   And round thee lies the smooth, untrodden snow,

---

* By permission of the Century Company, New York.

When naught is thine that made thee once so fair,
  I love to watch thy shadowy form below,
And through thy leafless arms to look above
On stars that brighter beam, when most we need
  their love.

THE GLORY OF THE WOODS*

BY SUSAN FENIMORE COOPER

OF THE infinite variety of fruits which spring from the bosom of the earth, the trees of the wood are greatest in dignity. Of all the works of the creation which know the changes of life and death, the trees of the forest have the longest existence. Of all the objects which crown the gray earth, the woods preserve unchanged, throughout the greatest reach of time, their native character. The works of man are ever varying their aspect; his towns and his fields alike reflect the unstable opinions, the fickle wills and fancies of each passing generation; but the forests on his borders remain to-day the same as they were ages of years since. Old as the everlasting hills, during thousands of seasons they have put forth and laid down their verdure in calm obedience to the decree which first bade them cover the ruins of the Deluge.

------

* By permission of the Baker and Taylor Company, New York.

THE AMERICAN FORESTS*

BY JOHN MUIR

THE forests of America, however slighted by man, must have been a great delight to God; for they were the best He had ever planted. The whole continent was a garden, and from the beginning it seemed to be favored above all the other wild parks and gardens of the globe. To prepare the ground, it was rolled and sifted in seas with infinite loving deliberation and forethought, lifted into the light, submerged and warmed over and over again, pressed and crumpled into folds and ridges, mountains and hills, subsoiled with heaving volcanic fires, plowed and ground and sculptured into scenery and soil with glaciers and rivers — every feature growing and changing from beauty to beauty, higher and higher. And in the fulness of time it was planted in groves, and belts, and broad, exuberant, mantling forests, with the largest, most varied, most fruitful, and most beautiful trees in the world. Bright seas made its border with wave embroidery and icebergs; gray deserts were outspread in the middle of it, mossy tundras on the north, savannas on the south, and blooming prairies and plains; while lakes and rivers shone through all the vast forests and openings, and happy birds and beasts

* By permission of the publishers, Houghton, Mifflin & Co.

gave delightful animation. Everywhere, everywhere over all the blessed continent, there were beauty, and melody, and kindly, wholesome, foodful abundance.

These forests were composed of about five hundred species of trees, all of them in some way useful to man, ranging in size from twenty-five feet in height and less than one foot in diameter at the ground, to four hundred feet in height and more than twenty feet in diameter —lordly monarchs proclaiming the gospel of beauty like apostles. For many a century after the ice-plows were melted, nature fed them and dressed them every day; working like a man, a loving, devoted, painstaking gardener; fingering every leaf and flower and mossy furrowed bole; bending, trimming, modeling, balancing, painting them with the loveliest colors; bringing over them now clouds with cooling shadows and showers, now sunshine; fanning them with gentle winds and rustling their leaves; exercising them in every fibre with storms, and pruning them; loading them with flowers and fruit, loading them with snow, and ever making them more beautiful as the years rolled by.

. . . .

In the settlement and civilization of the country; bread more than timber or beauty, was wanted; and in the blindness of hunger, the early settlers, claiming Heaven as their guide, regarded God's trees as only a larger kind of pernicious weeds, extremely hard to get rid of. Accordingly, with no eye to the future, these pious destroyers waged interminable forest wars; chips flew thick and fast; trees in their beauty fell crashing by millions, smashed to confusion, and the smoke of their burning has been rising to heaven more than two hundred years. After the Atlantic coast from Maine to Georgia had been mostly cleared and scorched into melancholy ruins, the overflowing multitude of bread and money seekers poured over the Alleghenies into the fertile Middle West, spreading ruthless devastation ever wider and farther over the rich valley of the Mississippi and the vast, shadowy pine region about the Great Lakes. Thence still westward the invading horde of destroyers, called settlers, made its fiery way over the broad Rocky Mountains, felling and burning more fiercely than ever, until at last it has reached the wild side of the continent, and entered the last of the great aboriginal forests on the shores of the Pacific.

Surely, then, it should not be wondered at that lovers of their country, bewailing its baldness, are now crying aloud: "Save what is left of the forests!" Clearing has surely now gone far enough; soon timber will be scarce, and not a grove will be left to rest in or pray in. The remnant protected will yield plenty of timber, a perennial harvest for every right use, without further diminution of its area, and will continue to cover the springs of the rivers that rise in the mountains and give irrigating waters to the dry valleys at their feet, prevent wasting floods, and be a blessing to everybody forever.

Every other civilized nation in the world has been compelled to care for its forests, and so we must if waste and destruction are not to go on to the bitter end, leaving America as barren as Palestine or Spain. In its calmer moments in the midst of bewildering hunger and war and restless over-industry, Prussia has learned that the forest plays an important part in human progress, and that the advance in civilization only makes it more indispensable. It has, therefore, as shown by Mr. Pinchot, refused to deliver its forests to more or less speedy destruction by permitting them to pass into private ownership. But the state woodlands are not allowed to lie idle. On the contrary, they are made to produce as much timber as is possible without spoiling them. In the administration of its forests, the state righteously considers itself bound to treat them as a trust for the nation as a whole, and to keep in view the common good of the people for all time.

In France no government forests have been sold since 1870. On the other hand, about one half of the fifty million francs spent on forestry has been given to engineering works, to make the replanting of denuded areas possible. The disappearance of the forests in the first place, it is claimed, may be traced in most cases directly to mountain pasturage.   The provisions of the code concerning private woodlands are substantially these: No private owner may clear his woodlands without giving notice to the government at least four months in advance, and the forest service may forbid the clearing on the following grounds: to maintain the soil on mountains, to defend the soil against erosion and flooding by rivers or torrents, to insure the existence of springs and watercourses, to protect the dunes and seashore, etc.   A proprietor who has cleared his forest without permission is subject to heavy fine, and in addition may be made to replant the cleared area.

In Switzerland, after many laws like our own had been found wanting, the Swiss forest school was established in 1865, and soon after the Federal Forest Law was enacted, which is binding over nearly two-thirds of the country.   Under its provisions, the cantons must appoint and pay the number of suitably educated foresters required for the fulfilment of the forest law; and in the organization of a normally stocked forest, the object of first importance must be the cutting each year of an amount of timber equal to the total annual increase, and no more.

The Russian government passed a law in 1888, declaring that clearing is forbidden in protected forests, and is allowed in others "only when its effects will not be to disturb the suitable relations which should exist between forest and agricultural lands."

Even Japan is ahead of us in the management of her forests. They cover an area of about 29,000,000 acres. The feudal lords valued the woodlands, and enacted vigorous protective laws; and when, in the latest civil war, the Mikado government destroyed the feudal system, it declared the forests that had belonged to the feudal lords to be the property of the state, promulgated a forest law binding on the whole kingdom, and founded a school of forestry in Tokio. The forest service does not rest satisfied with the present proportion of woodland, but looks to planting the best forest trees it can find in any country, if likely to be useful and to thrive in Japan.

In India systematic forest management was begun about forty years ago, under difficulties — presented by the character of the country, the prevalence of running fires, opposition from lumbermen, settlers, etc. — not unlike those which confront us now. Of the total area of government forests, perhaps 70,000,000 acres, 55,000,000 acres have been brought under the control of the forestry department — a larger area than that of all our national parks and reservations. The chief aims of the administration are effective protection of the forests from fire, an efficient system of regeneration and cheap transportation of the forest products; the results so far have been most beneficial and encouraging.

It seems, therefore, that almost every civilized nation can give us a lesson on the management and care of forests. So far our Government has done nothing effective with its forests, though the best in the world, but is like a rich and foolish spendthrift who has inherited a magnificent estate in perfect order, and then has left his rich fields and meadows, forests and parks, to be sold and plundered and wasted at will, depending on their inexhaustible abundance. Now it is plain that the forests are not inexhaustible, and that quick measures must be taken if ruin is to be avoided.   Year by year the remnant is growing smaller before the axe and fire, while the laws in existence provide neither for the protection of the timber from destruction nor for its use where it is most needed.

.   .   .   .

Notwithstanding all the waste and use which have been going on unchecked like a storm for more than two centuries, it is not yet too late, though it is high time, for the Government to begin a rational administration of its forests.   About seventy million acres it still owns — enough for all the country, if wisely used.   These residual forests are generally on mountain slopes, just where they are doing the most good, and where their removal would be followed by

the greatest number of evils; the lands they cover
are too rocky and high for agriculture, and can never
be made as valuable for any other crop as for the
present crop of trees. It has been shown over
and over again that if these mountains were to be
stripped of their trees and underbrush, and kept
bare and sodless by hordes of sheep and the innumerable fires the shepherds set, besides those of the
millmen, prospectors, shake-makers, and all sorts
of adventurers, both lowlands and mountains would
speedily become little better than deserts, compared
with their present beneficent fertility. During
heavy rainfalls and while the winter accumulations
of snow were melting, the larger streams would
swell into destructive torrents; cutting deep, rugged-
edged gullies, carrying away the fertile humus and
soil as well as sand and rocks, filling up and overflowing their lower channels, and covering the low-
land fields with raw detritus. Drought and barrenness would follow.

In their natural condition, or under wise management, keeping out destructive sheep, preventing
fires, selecting the trees that should be cut for lumber,
and preserving the young ones and the shrubs and
sod of herbaceous vegetation, these forests would be
a never-failing fountain of wealth and beauty.
The cool shades of the forest give rise to moist beds
and currents of air, and the sod of grasses and the
various flowering plants and shrubs thus fostered,

together with the network and sponge of tree roots, absorb and hold back the rain and the waters from melting snow, compelling them to ooze and percolate and flow gently through the soil in streams that never dry. All the pine needles and rootlets and blades of grass, and the fallen, decaying trunks of trees, are dams, storing the bounty of the clouds and dispensing it in perennial life-giving streams, instead of allowing it to gather suddenly and rush headlong in short-lived devastating floods. Everybody on the dry side of the continent is beginning to find this out, and, in view of the waste going on, is growing more and more anxious for Government protection. The outcries we hear against forest reservations come mostly from thieves who are wealthy and steal timber by wholesale. They have so long been allowed to steal and destroy in peace that any impediment to forest robbery is denounced as a cruel and irreligious interference with "vested rights," likely to endanger the repose of all ungodly welfare.

Gold, gold, gold! How strong a voice that metal has!

O wae for the siller, it is sae preva'lin'.

Even in Congress, a sizable chunk of gold, carefully concealed, will outtalk and outfight all the nation on a subject like forestry, well-smothered in ignorance, and in which the money interests of only a few are conspicuously involved. Under these circumstances, the bawling, blethering oratorical stuff drowns the voice of God Himself. Yet the dawn of a new day in forestry is breaking. Honest citizens see that only the rights of the Government are being trampled, not those of the settlers. Merely what belongs to all alike is reserved, and every acre that is left should be held together under the Federal Government as a basis for a general policy of administration for the public good. The people will not always be deceived by selfish opposition, whether from lumber and mining corporations or from sheepmen and prospectors, however cunningly brought forward underneath fables and gold.

Emerson says that things refuse to be mismanaged long. An exception would seem to be found in the case of our forests, which have been mismanaged rather long, and now come desperately near being like smashed eggs and spilt milk. Still, in the long run the world does not move backward. The wonderful advance made in the last few years, in creating four national parks in the West, and thirty forest reservations, embracing nearly forty million acres; and in the planting of the borders of streets and highways and spacious parks in all the great cities, to satisfy the natural taste and hunger for landscape beauty and righteousness that God has put, in some measure, into every human being and animal, shows the trend of awakening public opinion. The making of the far-famed New York Central Park was opposed by even good men, with misguided pluck, perseverance, and ingenuity, but straight right won its way, and now that park is appreciated. So we confidently believe it will be with our great national parks and forest reservations. There will be a period of indifference on the part of the rich, sleepy with wealth, and of the toiling millions, sleepy with poverty, most of whom never saw a forest; a period of screaming protest and objection from the plunderers, who are as unconscionable and enterprising as Satan. But light is surely coming, and the friends of destruction will preach and bewail in vain.

The United States Government has always been proud of the welcome it has extended to good men of every nation, seeking freedom and homes and bread. Let them be welcomed still as nature welcomes them, to the woods as well as to the prairies and plains. No place is too good for good men, and still there is room. They are invited to heaven, and may well be allowed in America. Every place is made better by them. Let them be as free to pick gold and gems from the hills, to cut and hew, dig and plant, for homes and bread, as the birds are to pick berries from the wild bushes, and moss and leaves for nests. The ground will be glad to feed them, and the pines will come down from the mountains for their homes as willingly as the cedars came from Lebanon for Solomon's temple. Nor will the woods be the worse for this use, or their benign influences be diminished any more than the sun is diminished by shining. Mere destroyers, however, tree-killers, spreading death and confusion in the fairest groves and gardens ever planted, let the Government hasten to cast them out and make an end of them. For it must be told again and again, and be burningly borne in mind, that just now, while protective measures are being deliberated languidly, destruction and use are speeding on faster and farther every day. The axe and saw are insanely busy, chips are flying thick as snowflakes, and every summer thousands of acres of priceless forests, with their underbrush, soil, springs, climate, scenery, and religion, are vanishing away in clouds of smoke, while, except in the national parks, not one forest guard is employed.

All sorts of local laws and regulations have been tried and found wanting, and the costly lessons of our experience, as well as that of every civilized nation, show exclusively that the fate of the remnant of our forests is in the hands of the Federal Government, and that if the remnant is to be saved at all, it must be saved quickly.

Any fool can destroy trees. They cannot run away; and if they could, they would still be destroyed — chased and hunted down as long as fun or a dollar could be got out of their bark hides, branching horns, or magnificent bole backbones. Few that fell trees plant them; nor would planting avail much toward getting back anything like the noble primeval forests. During a man's life only saplings can be grown, in the place of the old trees — tens of centuries old — that have been destroyed. It took more than three thousand years to make some of the trees in these Western woods — trees that are still standing in perfect strength and beauty, waving and singing in the mighty forests of the Sierra. Through all the wonderful, eventful centuries since Christ's time — and long before that — God has cared for these trees, saved them from drought, disease, avalanches, and a thousand straining, leveling tempests and floods; but He cannot save them from fools — only Uncle Sam can do that.

TALKING IN THEIR SLEEP*

BY EDITH M. THOMAS

"You think I am dead,"
The apple-tree said,
"Because I have never a leaf to show —
Because I stoop
And my branches droop,
And the dull gray mosses over me grow!
But I'm alive in trunk and shoot;
The buds of next May
I fold away —
But I pity the withered grass at my foot."

* By permission of the publishers, Houghton, Mifflin & Co.

"You think I am dead,"
The quick grass said,
"Because I have parted with stem and blade!
But under the ground
I am safe and sound,
With the snow's thick blanket over me laid.
I'm all alive, and ready to shoot
Should the spring of the year
Come dancing here —
But I pity the flower without branch or root."

"You think I am dead,"
A soft voice said,
"Because not a branch or root I own!
I never have died,
But close I hide
In a plumy seed that the wind has sown.
Patient I wait through the long winter hours;
You will see me again —
I shall laugh at you then,
Out of the eyes of a hundred flowers!"

———

THE FOREST

BY RICHARD JEFFERIES

From *The Open Air*

UNDER the trees the imagination plays unchecked,
and calls up the past as if yew bow and broad arrow

were still in the hunter's hands. So little is changed since then. The deer are here still. Sit down on the root of this oak (thinly covered with moss), and on that very spot it is quite possible a knight fresh home from the Crusades may have rested and feasted his eyes on the lovely green glades of his own unsurpassed England. The oak was there then, young and strong; it is here now, ancient, but sturdy. Rarely do you see an oak fall of itself. It decays to the last stump; it does not fall. The sounds are the same — the tap as a ripe acorn drops, the rustle of a leaf which comes down slowly, the quick rushes of mice playing in the fern. A movement at one side attracts the glance, and there is a squirrel darting about. There is another at the very top of the beech yonder out on the boughs, nibbling the nuts. A brown spot a long distance down the glade suddenly moves, and thereby shows itself to be a rabbit. The bellowing sound that comes now and then is from the stags, which are preparing to fight. The swine snort, and the mast and leaves rustle as they thrust them aside. So little is changed; these are the same sounds and the same movements, just as in the olden time.

The soft autumn sunshine, shorn of summer glare, lights up with color the fern, the fronds of which are yellow and brown, the leaves, the gray grass, and hawthorn sprays already turned. It seems as if the early morning's mists have the power of tinting leaf and fern, for so soon as they commence the green hues begin to disappear. There are swathes of fern yonder, cut down like grass or corn, the harvest of the forest. It will be used for litter and for thatching sheds. The yellow stalks — the stubble — will turn brown and wither through the winter, till the strong spring shoot comes up and the anemones flower. Though the sunbeams reach the ground here, half the green glade is in shadow, and for one step that you walk in sunlight ten are in shade. Thus, partly concealed in full day, the forest always contains a mystery. The idea that there may be something in the dim arches held up by the round columns of the beeches lures the foot-steps onward. Something must have been lately in the circle under the oak where the fern and bushes remain at a distance and wall in a lawn of green. There is nothing on the grass but the upheld leaves that have dropped, no mark of any creature, but this is not decisive; if there are no physical signs, there is a feeling that the shadow is not vacant. In the thickets, perhaps — the shadowy thickets with front of thorn — it has taken refuge and eluded us. Still onward the shadows lead us in vain but pleas-ant chase.

.   .   .   .

The oaks keep a circle round their base and stand at a majestic distance from each other, so that the wind and the sunshine enter, and their precincts are sweet and pleasant. The elms gather together, rubbing their branches in the gale till the bark is worn off and the boughs die; the shadow is deep under them, and moist, favorable to rank grass and coarse mushrooms. Beneath the ashes, after the first frost, the air is full of the bitterness of their blackened leaves, which have all come down at once. By the beeches there is little underwood, and the hollows are filled ankle-deep with their leaves. From the pines comes a fragrant odor, and thus the character of each group dominates the surrounding ground. The shade is too much for many flowers, which prefer the nooks of hedgerows. If there is no scope for the use of "express" rifles, this southern forest really is a forest and not an open hillside. It is a forest of trees, and there are no woodlands so beautiful and enjoyable as these, where it is possible to be lost a while without fear of serious consequences; where you can walk without stepping up to the waist in a decayed tree-trunk, or floundering in a bog; where neither venomous snake nor torturing mosquito causes constant apprehensions and constant irritation. To the eye there is nothing but beauty; to the imagination pleasant pageants of old time; to the ear the soothing cadence of the leaves as the gentle breeze goes over. The beeches rear their Gothic architecture; the oaks are planted firm like castles, unassailable. Quick squirrels climb and dart hither and thither, deer cross the distant glade, and, occasionally, a hawk passes like thought.

The something that may be in the shadow or the thicket, the vain, pleasant chase that beckons us on, still leads the footsteps from tree to tree, till by and by a lark sings, and, going to look for it, we find the stubble outside the forest — stubble still bright with the blue and white flowers of gray speedwell. One of the earliest to bloom in the spring, it continues till the plow comes again in autumn. Now looking back from the open stubble on the high wall of trees, the touch of autumn here and there is the more visible — oaks dotted with brown, horse chestnuts yellow, maples orange, and the bushes beneath red with haws.

THE VOICE OF THE PINE*

BY RICHARD WATSON GILDER

'Tis night upon the lake. Our bed of boughs
Is built where, high above, the pine-tree soughs.
'Tis still — and yet what woody noises loom
Against the background of the silent gloom!
One well might hear the opening of a flower
If day were hushed as this. A mimic shower
Just shaken from a branch, how large it sounded,
As 'gainst our canvas roof its three drops bounded!

* By permission of the Century Company, New York.

Across the rumpling waves the hoot-owl's bark
Tolls forth the midnight hour upon the dark.
What mellow booming from the hills doth come?
The mountain quarry strikes its mighty drum.

Long had we lain beside our pine-wood fire,
From things of sport our talk had risen higher.
How frank and intimate the words of men
When tented lonely in some forest glen!
No dallying now with masks, from whence emerges
Scarce one true feature forth.   The night-wind urges
To straight and simple speech.   So we had thought
Aloud; no secrets but to light were brought.
The hid and spiritual hopes, the wild,
Unreasoned longings that, from child to child,
Mortals still cherish (though with modern shame) —
To these, and things like these, we gave a name;
And as we talked, the intense and resinous fire
Lit up the towering boles, till nigh and nigher
They gathered round, a ghostly company,
Like beasts who seek to know what men may be.

Then to our hemlock beds, but not to sleep—
For listening to the stealthy steps that creep
About the tent, or falling branch, but most
A noise was like the rustling of a host,
Or like the sea that breaks upon the shore —
It was the pine-tree's murmur.   More and more
It took a human sound.   These words I felt
Into the skyey darkness float and melt:

"Heardst thou these wanderers reasoning of a time
When men more near the Eternal One shall climb?
How like the new-born child, who cannot tell
A mother's arm that wraps it warm and well!
Leaves of His rose; drops in His sea that flow —
Are they, alas! so blind they may not know
Here, in this breathing world of joy and fear,
They can no nearer get to God than here?"

FORMS AND EXPRESSIONS OF TREES

BY WILSON FLAGG

THE different forms of trees, and their endless variety of foliage and spray, have, from the earliest times, been favorite studies of the painter and the naturalist. Not only has each species certain distinguishing marks, but their specific characters are greatly modified in individual trees. The Psalmist compares a godly man to a tree that is planted by rivers of water, whose leaf shall not wither — seeing in the stateliness and beauty of such a tree an emblem of the noble virtues of the human heart. Trees are distinguished by their grandeur or their elegance, by their primness or their grace, by the stiffness of their leaves and branches, or by their waving and tremulous motions. Some stand forth as if in defiance of the wind and the tempest; others, with long, drooping branches, find security in bending to the gale, like the slender herbs in the meadow.

Trees are generally classed as landscape ornaments, according to their general outlines. "Some trees ascend vertically," says St. Pierre, "and having arrived at a certain height, in an air perfectly unobstructed, fork off in various tiers, and send out their branches horizontally, like an apple-tree; or incline them toward the earth, like a fir; or hollow them in the form of a cup, like the sassafras; or round them into the shape of a mushroom, like the pine; or straighten them into a pyramid, like the poplar; or roll them as wool upon the distaff, like the cypress; or suffer them to float at the discretion of the winds, like the birch." These are the normal varieties in the shape of trees. Others may be termed accidental, like those of the tall and imperfectly developed trees, which have been cramped by growing in dense assemblages, and of the pollards that have issued from the stumps and roots of other trees.

Trees are generally wanting in that kind of beauty which we admire in a vase, or an elegant piece of furniture. They have more of those qualities we look for in a picture and in the ruder works of architecture. Nature is neither geometrical nor precise in her delineations. She betrays a design in all her works, but never casts two objects in the same mold. She does not paint by formulas, nor build by square and compass, nor plant by a line and dibble; she takes no note of formal arrangements, or of the "line of beauty," or of direct adaptation of means to ends. She shakes all things together, as in a dice-box, and as they fall out there they remain, growing crooked or straight, mean or magnificent, beautiful or ugly, but adapted by the infinite variety of their forms and dispositions to the wants and habits of all creatures.

The beauty of trees is something that exists chiefly in our imagination. We admire them for their evident adaptation to purposes of shade and shelter. Some of them we regard as symbols or images of a fine poetic sentiment. Such are the slender willows and poplars, that remind us of grace and refinement, becoming the emblems of some agreeable moral affection, or the embodiment of some striking metaphor. Thus Coleridge personifies the white birch as the "Lady of the Woods," and the oak by other poets is called the monarch, and the ash the Venus of the forest. The weeping willow, beautiful on account of its graceful spray, becomes still more so when regarded as the emblem of sorrow. The oak, in like manner, is interesting as the symbol of strength and fortitude. A young fir-tree always reminds us of primness; hence the name spruce, which is applied to many of the species, is a word used to express formality. The cedar of Lebanon would be viewed by all with a certain romantic interest, on account of the frequent mention of it in

Holy Writ, as well as for its nobleness of dimensions and stature.

It is with certain interesting scenes in the romance of travel that we associate the palms of the tropics. They have acquired singular attractions by appearing frequently in scenes that represent the life and manners of the simple inhabitants of the equatorial regions. We see them in pictures bending their fan-like heads majestically over the humble hut of the Indian, supplying him at once with milk, bread, and fruit, and affording him the luxury of their shade. They emblemize the beneficence of nature, which, by means of their products, supplies the wants of man before he has learned the arts of civilized life.

Writers in general apply the term "picturesque" to trees which are devoid of symmetry and very irregular in their outlines, either crooked from age or from some natural eccentricity of growth. Thus the tupelo is so called, to distinguish it from round-headed and symmetrical or beautiful trees. This distinction is not very precise; but it is sanctioned by general use, and answers very well for common purposes of vague description. I shall use the words in a similar manner, not adhering to the distinction as philosophical. Indeed, it is impossible to find words that will clearly express a complex idea. Words are very much like tunes played on a jew's-harp; the notes intended to be given by the performer are accompanied by the louder ring of the keynote of the instrument, making it difficult to detect the notes of the tune, except in the hands of an extraordinary performer.

Nature has provided against the disagreeable effects that would result from the dismemberment of trees, by giving to those which are the most common a great irregularity of outline, admitting of disproportion without deformity. Symmetry in the forms of natural objects becomes wearisome by making too great a demand upon the attention required for observing the order and relations of the different parts. But if the objects in the landscape be irregular, both in their forms and their distribution, we make no effort to attend to the relations of parts to the whole, because no such harmony is indicated. Such a scene has the beauty of repose. The opposite effect is observed in works of architecture, in which irregularity puzzles the mind to discover the mutual relations of parts, and becomes disagreeable by disturbing our calculation and disappointing our curiosity. The charm of art is variety combined with uniformity; the charm of nature is variety without uniformity. Nature speaks to us in prose, art in verse.

Though we always admire a perfectly symmetrical oak or elm, because such perfection is rare, it will be admitted that the irregular forms of trees are more productive of agreeable impressions on the mind. The oak, one of the most interesting of all trees, is, in an important sense, absolutely ugly, especially when old age has increased its picturesque attractions. Indeed, if we could always reason correctly on the subjects of our consciousness, we should find that a very small part of that complex quality which we call beauty yields any organic pleasure to the sight. The charm of most of the objects in this category exists only in our imaginations. In trees and the general objects of the landscape we look neither for symmetry nor proportion; the absence of these qualities is, therefore, never disagreeable. It is the nonfulfilment of some expectation, or the apparently imperfect supply of some important want, that offends the sight, as when a conspicuous gap occurs in some finely proportioned work of art.

SONG

BY THOMAS LOVE PEACOCK

FOR the tender beech and the sapling oak,
  That grow by the shadowy rill,
You may cut down both at a single stroke,
  You may cut down which you will.

But this you must know, that as long as they grow,
  Whatever change may be,
You can never teach either oak or beech
  To be aught but a greenwood tree.

A FRANK AVOWAL

BY N. P. WILLIS

From *Outdoors at Idlewild*

I SAID, just now, that I had not yet planted a single tree at Idlewild. This is half a betrayal of a weakness that I feel growing upon me; and, having been reminded to-day of what I have once put in print from quite an opposite feeling, I may as well make a clean breast, and so, perhaps, get the better of it. In our current of life we have eddies of these quiet side-weaknesses — a string of them. At fourteen we begin to be secretly nervous lest our beard should be belated. Whiskers pretty well outlined, there awakens an unconfessed wonder and indignation that the world does not seem ready for our particular genius. Soon after, we are mortified that even our guardian angel, reading our hearts, should know how hard it is to smile with contempt because papas do not think us "a good match." The struggle of life comes; and, with the current swifter and deeper, there is an interval, perhaps, when the eddies of secret weakness find no slack-water for play. But, that past, we begin to be sensitive about our age and our first gray hairs; and when that is scarce over, there comes another feeling — the weakness that I speak of — the secret reason (though scarce before recognized and brought fairly to the light) why I have been two years molding Idlewild into a home, and have not yet set out a tree.

———

I SAW IN LOUISIANA A LIVE-OAK GROWING*

BY WALT WHITMAN

I SAW in Louisiana a live-oak growing,
All alone stood it and the moss hung down from the
 branches,
Without any companion it grew there uttering
 joyous leaves of dark green,
And its look, rude, unbending, lusty, made me think
 of myself,
But I wonder'd how it could utter joyous leaves
 standing alone there without its friend near,
 for I knew I could not,
And I broke off a twig with a certain number of
 leaves upon it, and twined around it a little
 moss,
And brought it away, and I have placed it in sight
 in my room.
It is not needed to remind me of my own dear
 friends
(For I believe lately I think of little else than of
 them),

* From "Poetical Works," published by David McKay, Philadelphia, Pa.

Yet it remains to me a curious token, it makes me
 think of manly love;
For all that, and though the live-oak glistens there
 in Louisiana, solitary in a wide, flat space,
Uttering joyous leaves all its life without a friend,
 a lover near,
I know very well I could not.

THE MAPLE*

BY JAMES RUSSELL LOWELL

THE Maple puts her corals on in May,
While loitering frosts about the lowlands cling,
To be in tune with what the robins sing,
Plastering new log-huts 'mid her branches gray;
But when the Autumn southward turns away,
Then in her veins burns most the blood of
 Spring,
And every leaf, intensely blossoming,
Makes the year's sunset pale the set of day.
O Youth unprescient, were it only so
With trees you plant, and in whose shade reclined,
Thinking their drifting blooms Fate's coldest
 snow,
You carve dear names upon the faithful rind,
Nor in that vernal stem the cross foreknow
That Age shall bear, silent, yet unresigned!

* By permission of the publishers, Houghton, Mifflin & Co.

UNDER THE GREENWOOD TREE

BY WILLIAM SHAKESPEARE

UNDER the greenwood tree
Who loves to lie with me,
And tune his merry note
Unto the sweet bird's throat —
Come hither, come hither, come hither!
Here shall we see
No enemy
But winter and rough weather.

Who doth ambition shun,
And loves to live i' the sun,
Seeking the food he eats,
And pleased with what he gets —
Come hither, come hither, come hither!
Here shall he see
No enemy
But winter and rough weather.

THE LESSON OF A TREE*

BY WALT WHITMAN

I SHOULD not take either the biggest or the most picturesque tree to illustrate it. Here is one of my favorites now before me, a fine yellow poplar, quite

* From "Prose Works," published by David McKay, Philadelphia, Pa.

straight, perhaps ninety feet high, and four thick
at the butt. How strong, vital, enduring! How
dumbly eloquent! What suggestions of imper-
turbability and *being*, as against the human trait of
mere *seeming*. Then the qualities, almost emo-
tional, palpably artistic, heroic, of a tree; so innocent and harmless, yet so savage. It *is*, yet says
nothing. How it rebukes, by its tough and equable
serenity, all weathers, this gusty-tempered little
whiffet, man, that runs indoors at a mite of rain
or snow. Science (or rather half-way science)
scoffs at reminiscence of dryad and hamadryad, and
of trees speaking. But, if they don't, they do as
well as most speaking, writing, poetry, sermons —
or rather they do a great deal better. I should say
indeed that those old dryad reminiscences are quite
as true as any, and profounder than most reminiscences we get. ("Cut this out," as the quack
mediciners say, and keep by you.) Go and sit in
a grove or woods, with one or more of those voice-
less companions, and read the foregoing and think.

THE BEAUTY OF TREES

BY WILSON FLAGG

IT IS difficult to realize how great a part of all
that is cheerful and delightful in the recollections
of our own life is associated with trees. They are

allied with the songs of morn, with the quiet of noonday, with social gatherings under the evening sky, and with all the beauty and attractiveness of every season. Nowhere does nature look more lovely, or the sounds from birds and insects, and from inanimate things, affect us more deeply, than in their benevolent shade. Never does the blue sky appear more serene than when its dappled azure glimmers through their green trembling leaves. Their shades, which, in the early ages, were the temples of religion and philosophy, are still the favorite resort of the studious, the scene of healthful sport for the active and adventurous, and the very sanctuary of peaceful seclusion for the contemplative and sorrowful.

THE SNOWING OF THE PINES*

BY THOMAS WENTWORTH HIGGINSON

SOFTER than silence, stiller than still air,
Float down from high pine-boughs the slender leaves.
The forest floor its annual boon receives
That comes like snowfall, tireless, tranquil, fair.
Gently they glide, gently they clothe the bare
Old rocks with grace. Their fall a mantle weaves
Of paler yellow than autumnal sheaves
Or those strange blossoms the witch-hazels wear.

* By permission of the publishers, Houghton, Mifflin & Co.

Athwart long aisles the sunbeams pierce their way;
High up, the crows are gathering for the night;
The delicate needles fill the air; the jay
Takes through their golden mist his radiant flight;
They fall and fall, till at November's close
The snowflakes drop as lightly — snows on snows.

MEN AND TREES*

BY EDITH M. THOMAS

SOME time since, on an enchanted summer afternoon, I heard the woods utter the following complaint, in tones half whisper, half musical recitative (I do not think I could have been asleep):

We that sway the forest realm,
Oak and chestnut, beech and elm,
Do grow weary standing here
Year by year — long year by year!
Will it never more befall us
We shall hear a master call us,
When our troops shall break their trance
And be joined in nimble dance?
He should lead us up and down,
Drunk with joy from root to crown,
Through the valley, over hill,
Servants unto music's will;
Leaf and nut the earth bestrewing,
Birds their truant nests pursuing —
Merry madness all around
In the trembling air and ground!

* By permission of the publishers, Houghton, Mifflin & Co.

So it chanced (our sages say)
In the bard Amphion's day;
But since he was lost to earth,
None could wake our souls to mirth.
Music, music, music bring,
Blow on flute, and smite the string!
We for revel fare are ripe —
We would dance, but who will pipe?
Now the best of bards alive
In his art so ill doth thrive,
He might try for days together,
And not start one plume of heather.

Truth to say, the only Amphionic music the trees hear nowadays is the ring of the woodman's axe, their only dance a short, giddy reel.

There are spirits of the sylvan and spirits of the open, natural interpreters of the woods and interpreters of the fields. The true spiritual descendants of the Druids are a small minority. How many of us, while loving trees, are also lovers of the mid-forest and deep shade? If not lost in the woods, we are much at a loss there. The surrounding is alien. A latent timorousness akin to superstition starts up and walks with us, advising:

Of forests and enchantments drear,
Where more is meant than meets the ear.

This under-meaning or over-meaning of the woods still baffles. Their most gracious invitation and salutation at a little distance are never quite made good when I have stepped across their precincts. Foretaste of their indifference has often kept me a traveler "all around Robin Hood's barn," rather than through it. Or is it that, not greatly fond of interiors (of woodland interiors, even), I prefer to stand or sit in the strong-pillared portico, and gaze thence far into the mysterious presence-filled sanctuary? Were I within, the preached word would but puzzle my child-like capacity. Such impression I have of the woods in full leaf, roofed over and curtained round. In winter, in early spring, or in late autumn, when the sky's good light keeps me in countenance, my wood-wit is less dull. Looking sunward through these long aisles, I see the dead leaves repeatedly lifted on the awakening wind. The ground itself seems to acquire motion from their fluctuations, and appears now rising, now subsiding, as the wind comes or goes. Are the leaves surely dead? Near by they have a cautionary speech all their own, a continuous "hist" and "'sh" — sounds distinct from the sonorous wind-march through the tree-tops. Soul of the forest and of all sylvan summers gone, set free by the blown ripe leaves — I flush it, and follow it through the shrill woods!

THE WAYSIDE INN — AN APPLE TREE
FROM THE GERMAN

I HALTED at a pleasant inn,
    As I my way was wending —
A golden apple was the sign,
    From knotty bough depending.

Mine host — it was an apple tree —
 He smilingly received me,
And spread his sweetest, choicest fruit
 To strengthen and relieve me.

Full many a little feathered guest
 Came through his branches springing;
They hopped and flew from spray to spray,
 Their notes of gladness singing.

Beneath his shade I laid me down,
 And slumber sweet possessed me;
The soft wind blowing through the leaves
 With whispers low caressed me.

And when I rose and would have paid
 My host, so open-hearted,
He only shook his lofty head —
 I blessed him and departed.

FOREST HYMN

BY WILLIAM CULLEN BRYANT

THE groves were God's first temples. **Ere man**
 learned
To hew the shaft, and lay the architrave,
And spread the roof above them — ere he framed
The lofty vault to gather and roll back
The sound of anthems — in the darkling wood,

Amidst the cool and silence, he knelt down
And offered to the Mightiest solemn thanks
And supplications.

For his simple heart
Might not resist the sacred influences
That, from the stilly twilight of the place,
And from the gray old trunks that high in heaven
Mingled their mossy boughs, and from the sound
Of the invisible breath that swayed at once
All their green tops, stole over him, and bowed
His spirit with the thought of boundless Power
And inaccessible Majesty.

Ah! why
Should we, in the world's riper years, neglect
God's ancient sanctuaries, and adore
Only among the crowd, and under roofs
That our frail hands have raised? Let me, at least,
Here, in the shadow of this aged wood,
Offer one hymn, thrice happy if it find
Acceptance in his ear.

Father, Thy hand
Hath reared these venerable columns: Thou
Didst weave this verdant roof. Thou didst look down
Upon the naked earth, and forthwith rose
All these fair ranks of trees. They in Thy sun
Budded, and shook their green leaves in Thy breeze,
And shot toward heaven. The century-living crow,

Whose birth was in their tops, grew old and died
Among their branches; till at last they stood,
As now they stand, massy, and tall, and dark —
Fit shrine for humble worshiper to hold
Communion with his Maker.

        Here are seen
No traces of man's pomp or pride; no silks
Rustle, no jewels shine, nor envious eyes
Encounter; no fantastic carvings show
The boast of our vain race to change the form
Of thy fair works. But Thou art here; Thou fill'st
The solitude. Thou art in the soft winds
That run along the summits of these trees
In music; Thou art in the cooler breath
That from the inmost darkness of the place
Comes scarcely felt; the barky trunks, the grouna,
The fresh, moist ground, are all instinct with Thee.

Here is continual worship; nature, here,
In the tranquillity that Thou dost love,
Enjoys thy presence. Noiselessly around
From perch to perch, the solitary bird
Passes; and yon clear spring, that midst its herbs
Wells softly forth, and visits the strong roots
Of half the mighty forest, tells no tale
Of all the good it does.

        Thou hast not left
Thyself without a witness, in these shades,

Of Thy perfections. Grandeur, strength, and grace
Are here to speak of Thee. This mighty oak —
By whose immovable stem I stand, and seem
Almost annihilated — not a prince
In all the proud Old World beyond the deep
E'er wore his crown as loftily as he
Wears the green coronal of leaves with which
Thy hand has graced him.

          Nestled at his root
Is beauty such as blooms not in the glare
Of the broad sun. That delicate forest-flower,
With scented breath and look so like a smile,
Seems, as it issues from the shapeless mold,
An emanation of the indwelling Life,
A visible token of the upholding Love,
That are the soul of this wide universe,

My heart is awed within me when I think
Of the great miracle that still goes on
In silence round me — the perpetual work
Of Thy creation, finished, yet renewed
Forever. Written on Thy works I read
The lesson of Thy own eternity.
Lo! all grow old and die; but see again
How, on the faltering footsteps of decay,
Youth presses — ever gay and beautiful youth —
In all its beautiful forms. These lofty trees
Wave not less proudly than their ancestors
Molder beneath them.

Oh, there is not lost
One of earth's charms: upon her bosom **yet**,
After the flight of untold centuries,
The freshness of her fair beginning lies,
And yet shall lie.   Life mocks the idle hate
Of his arch-enemy Death; yea, seats himself
Upon the sepulchre, and blooms and smiles,
And of the triumphs of his ghastly foe
Makes his own nourishment.   For he came forth
From Thine own bosom, and shall have no end.

There have been holy men who hid themselves
Deep in the woody wilderness, and gave
Their lives to thought and prayer, till they outlived
The generation born with them, nor seemed
Less aged than the hoary trees and rocks
Around them; and there have been holy men
Who deemed it were not well to pass life thus.
But let me often to these solitudes
Retire, and in Thy presence reassure
My feeble virtue.   Here its enemies,
The passions, at Thy plainer footsteps shrink
And tremble, and are still.

O God! when Thou
Dost scare the world with tempests, set on fire
The heavens with falling thunder-bolts, or fill,
With all the waters of the firmament,
The swift, dark whirlwind that uproots the woods

And drowns the villages; when, at Thy call,
Uprises the great deep and throws himself
Upon the continent, and overwhelms
Its cities; who forgets not, at the sight
Of these tremendous tokens of Thy power,
His pride, and lays his strifes and follies by?

Oh, from these sterner aspects of Thy face
Spare me and mine; nor let us need the wrath
Of the mad, unchained elements to teach
Who rules them.   Be it ours to mediate,
In these calm shades, Thy milder majesty,
And to the beautiful order of Thy works
Learn to conform the order of our lives.

———

FROM

HAROLD THE DAUNTLESS

BY SIR WALTER SCOTT

'Tis merry in greenwood, thus runs the old lay,
In the gladsome month of lively May,
When the wild bird's song on stem and spray
     Invites to forest bower;
Then rears the ash his airy crest
Then shines the birch in silver vest,
And the beech in glistening leaves is drest,
And dark between shows the oak's proud breast,
     Like a chieftain's frowning tower.

THE MAJESTY OF TREES
BY WASHINGTON IRVING

THERE is a serene and settled majesty in woodland scenery that enters into the soul, and delights and elevates it, and fills it with noble inclinations. As the leaves of trees are said to absorb all noxious qualities of the air and to breathe forth a purer atmosphere, so it seems to me as if they drew from us all sordid and angry passions, and breathed forth peace and philanthropy.

There is something nobly simple and pure in a taste for the cultivation of forest trees. It argues I think, a sweet and generous nature to have this strong relish for the beauties of vegetation, and this friendship for the hardy and glorious sons of the forest. There is a grandeur of thought connected with this part of rural economy. It is, if I may be allowed the figure, the heroic line of husbandry. It is worthy of liberal, and free-born, and aspiring men. He who plants an oak, looks forward to future ages, and plants for posterity. Nothing can be less selfish than this.

A FAMOUS COUPLET
BY ALEXANDER POPE

'TIS education forms the common mind;
Just as the twig is bent the tree's inclined.

A FEW OLD PROVERBS

ANONYMOUS

"If the Oak is out before the Ash,
'Twill be a summer of wet and splash;
If the Ash is out before the Oak,
'Twill be a summer of fire and smoke."

"When the Hawthorn bloom too early shows,
We shall have still many snows."

"When the Oak puts on his goslings gray
'Tis time to sow barley night or day."

"When Elm leaves are big as a shilling,
Plant kidney beans if you are willing;
When Elm leaves are as big as a penny,
You *must* plant beans if you wish to have any."

———

HISTORIC TREES

BY ALEXANDER SMITH

I DO not wonder that great earls value their trees and never, save in the direst extremity, lift upon them the axe. Ancient descent and glory are made audible in the proud murmur of immemorial woods. There are forests in England whose leafy noises

may be shaped into Agincourt, and the names of
the battlefields of the Roses; oaks that dropped
their acorns in the year that Henry VIII. held his
field of the Cloth of Gold, and beeches that gave
shelter to the deer when Shakespeare was a boy.
There they stand, in sun and shower, the broad-
armed witnesses of perished centuries; and sore must
his need be who commands a woodland massacre.
A great tree, the rings of a century in its boll, is one
of the noblest of natural objects; and it touches the
imagination no less than the eye, for it grows out of
tradition and a past order of things, and is pathetic
with the suggestions of dead generations. Trees
waving a colony of rooks in the wind to-day are
older than historic lines. Trees are your best
antiques. There are cedars on Lebanon which the
axes of Solomon spared, they say, when he was busy
with his Temple; there are olives on Olivet that
might have rustled in the ears of the Master of the
Twelve; there are oaks in Sherwood which have
tingled to the horn of Robin Hood, and have listened to Maid Marian's laugh. Think of an existing Syrian cedar which is nearly as old as history,
which was middle-aged before the wolf suckled
Romulus; think of an existing English elm in whose
branches the heron was reared which the hawks
of Saxon Harold killed! If you are a notable, and
wish to be remembered, better plant a tree than
build a city or strike a medal — it will outlast both.

THE OAK*

BY JAMES RUSSELL LOWELL

WHAT gnarlèd stretch, what depth of shade, is his!
  There needs no crown to mark the forest's
      king;
How in his leaves outshines full summer's bliss
  Sun, storm, rain, dew, to him their tribute bring.
How doth his patient strength the rude March
      wind
  Persuade to seem glad breaths of summer breeze,
And win the soil that fain would be unkind,
  To swell his revenues with proud increase!
So, from oft converse with life's wintry gales,
  Should man learn how to clasp with tougher
      roots
The inspiring earth; how otherwise avails
  The leaf-creating sap that upward shoots?

Lord! all thy works are lessons; each contains
  Some emblem of man's all-containing soul;
Shall he make fruitless all thy glorious pains,
  Delving within thy grace, an eyeless mole?
Make me the least of thy Dodona grove,
  Cause me some message of thy truth to bring,
Speak but a word through me, nor let thy love
  Among my boughs disdain to perch and sing.

*By permission of the publishers, Houghton, Mifflin & Co.

A TRUE NOBLEMAN

BY WASHINGTON IRVING

THERE is an affinity between all natures, animate and inanimate. The oak in the pride and lustihood of its growth, seems to me to take its range with the lion and the eagle, and to assimilate, in the grandeur of its attributes, to heroic and intellectual man. With its lofty pillar rising straight and direct toward heaven, bearing up its leafy honors from the impurities of earth, and supporting them aloft in free air and glorious sunshine, it is an emblem of what a *true nobleman* should be: a refuge for the weak, a shelter for the oppressed, a defense for the defenseless; warding off from the peltings of the storm, or the scorching rays of arbitrary power. He who is this is an ornament and a blessing to his native land. He who is otherwise abuses his eminent advantages — abuses the grandeur and prosperity which he has drawn from the bosom of his country. Should tempests arise, and he be laid prostrate by the storm, who would mourn over his fall? Should he be borne down by the oppressive hand of power, who would murmur at his fate? "WHY CUMBERETH HE THE GROUN ?"

THE OAK

BY JOHN DRYDEN

THE monarch *oak*, the patriarch of the trees,
Shoots slowly up, and spreads by slow degrees;
Three centuries he grows, and three he stays
Supreme in state, and in three more decays.

THE TREE

BY BJÖRNSTJERNE BJÖRNSON

THE tree's early leaf-buds were bursting their
brown.
"Shall I take them away?" said the frost, sweep-
ing down.
"No; leave them alone
Till the blossoms have grown,"
Prayed the tree, while he trembled from rootlet to
crown.

The tree bore his blossoms, and all the birds
sung.
"Shall I take them away?" said the wind, as he
swung.
"No leave them alone
Till the berries have grown,"
Said the tree, while his leaflets quivering hung.

The tree bore his fruit in the midsummer glow.
Said the child, "May I gather thy berries now?"
    "Yes; all thou canst see;
    Take them; all are for thee,"
Said the tree, while he bent down his laden boughs
    low.

FROM
THE FAUN*

BY RICHARD HOVEY

Hist! there's a stir in the brush.
Was it a face through the leaves?
Back of the laurels a scurry and rush
Hillward, then silence, except for the thrush
That throws one song from the dark of the bush
And is gone; and I plunge in the wood, and the
    swift soul cleaves
Through the swirl and the flow of the leaves,
As a swimmer stands with his white limbs
    bare to the sun
For the space that a breath is held, and drops in
    the sea;
And the undulant woodland folds round me, intimate
    fluctuant, free,
Like the clasp and the cling of waters, and the
    reach and the effort is done;
There is only the glory of living, exultant to be.

Oh, goodly damp smell of the ground!
Oh, rough, sweet bark of the trees!
Oh, clear, sharp cracklings of sound!
Oh, life that's a-thrill and a-bound
With the vigor of boyhood and morning and the
noontide's rapture of ease!

Was there ever a weary heart in the world?
A lag in the body's urge, or a flag of the spirit's
wings?
Did a man's heart ever break
For a lost hope's sake?
For here there is lilt in the quiet and calm in the
quiver of things.
Ay, this old oak, gray-grown and knurled,
Solemn and sturdy and big,
Is as young of heart, as alert and elate in his rest,
As the oriole there that clings to the tip of the twig
And scolds at the wind that it buffets too rudely
his nest.

IN THE HEMLOCKS*

BY JOHN BURROUGHS

From *Wake-Robin*

THE ancient hemlocks, whither I propose to
take the reader, are rich in many things beside
birds. Indeed, their wealth in this respect is owing

*By permission of the publishers, Houghton, Mifflin & Co.

mainly, no doubt, to their rank vegetable growths, their fruitful swamps, and their dark, sheltered retreats.

Their history is of an heroic cast. Ravished and torn by the tanner in his thirst for bark, preyed upon by the lumberman, assaulted and beaten back by the settler, still their spirit has never been broken, their energies never paralyzed. Not many years ago a public highway passed through them, but it was at no time a tolerable road; trees fell across it, mud and limbs choked it up, till finally travelers took the hint and went around; and now, walking along its deserted course, I see only the footprints of coons, foxes, and squirrels.

Nature loves such woods, and places her own seal upon them. Here she shows what can be done with ferns and mosses and lichens. The soil is marrowy and full of innumerable forests. Standing in these fragrant aisles, I feel the strength of the vegetable kingdom, and am awed by the deep and inscrutable processes of life going on so silently about me.

No hostile forms with axe or spud now visit these solitudes. The cows have half-hidden ways through them, and know where the best browsing is to be had. In the spring the farmer repairs to their bordering of maples to make sugar; in July and August women and boys from all the country about penetrate the old Barkpeelings for raspberries and blackberries; and I know a youth who wonderingly follows their languid stream, casting for trout.

———

ENGLISH WOODS AND AMERICAN*

BY JOHN BURROUGHS

From *Fresh Fields*

THE pastoral or field life of nature in England is so rank and full, that no woods or forests that I was able to find could hold their own against it for a moment. It flooded them like a tide. The grass grows luxuriantly in the thick woods, and where the grass fails, the coarse bracken takes its place. There was no wood spirit, no wildwood air. Our forests shut their doors against the fields; they shut out the strong light and the heat. Where the land has been long cleared, the woods put out a screen of low branches, or else a brushy growth starts up along their borders that guards and protects their privacy. Lift or part away these branches, and step inside, and you are in another world; new plants, new flowers, new birds, new animals, new insects, new sounds, new odors; in fact, an entirely different atmosphere and presence. Dry leaves cover the ground, delicate ferns and mosses drape the rocks, shy, delicate flowers gleam out here and there, the slender brown wood-frog leaps nimbly away from

*By permission of the publishers, Houghton, Mifflin & Co.

your feet, the little red newt fills its infantile pipe,
or hides under a leaf, the ruffed grouse bursts up
before you, the gray squirrel leaps from tree to tree,
the wood pewee utters its plaintive cry, the little
warblers lisp and dart amid the branches, and
sooner or later the mosquito demands his fee.
Our woods suggest new arts, new pleasures, a
new mode of life.   English parks and groves, when
the sun shines, suggest a perpetual picnic, or
Maying party; but no one, I imagine, thinks of
camping out in English woods.   The constant
rains, the darkened skies, the low temperature,
make the interior of a forest as uninviting as
an underground passage.   I wondered what
became of the dry leaves that are such a feature
and give out such a pleasing odor in our woods.
They are probably raked up and carried away;
or, if left upon the ground, are quickly resolved
into mold by the damp climate.

NATURE*

BY HENRY DAVID THOREAU

O NATURE! I do not aspire
To be the highest in thy quire —
To be a meteor in the sky,
Or comet that may range on high;

----

*By permission of the publishers, Houghton, Mifflin & Co.

Only a zephyr that may blow
Among the reeds by the river low;
Give me thy most privy place
Where to run my airy race.

In some withdrawn, unpublic mead
Let me sigh upon a reed,
Or in the woods, with leafy din,
Whisper the still evening in:
Some still work give me to do —
Only — be it near to you!

For I'd rather be thy child
And pupil, in the forest wild,
Than be the king of men elsewhere,
And most sovereign slave of care:
To have one moment of thy dawn,
Than share the city's year forlorn.

THE LITTLE LEAF

BY HENRY WARD BEECHER

ONCE on a time a little leaf was heard to sigh and cry, as leaves often do when a gentle wind is about. And the twig said:

"What is the matter, little leaf?"

"The wind," said the leaf, "just told me that one day it would pull me off, and throw me down to the ground to die!"

The twig told it to the branch on which it grew, and the branch told it to the tree. And when the tree heard it, it rustled all over, and sent word back to the leaf.

"Do not be afraid, hold on tightly, and you shall not go till you want to." And so the leaf stopped sighing and went on rustling and singing. And when the bright days of autumn came, the little leaf saw all the leaves around becoming very beautiful. Some were yellow and some were scarlet, and some were striped with both colors. Then it asked the tree what it meant. And the tree said:

"All these leaves are getting ready to fly away, and they have put on these beautiful colors because of joy."

Then the little leaf began to want to go, and grew very beautiful in thinking of it, and when it was very gay in colors, it saw that the branches of the tree had no color in them, and so the leaf said:

"O branch, why are you lead-colored and we golden?"

"We must keep on our work clothes," said the tree, "for our life is not done yet, but your clothes are for a holiday, because your task is over."

Just then a puff of wind came, and the leaf let go without thinking of it, and the wind took it up and turned it over and over, and then whirled it like a spark of fire in the air, and let it fall gently down

under the edge of the fence among hundreds of
leaves, and it fell into a dream and never waked up
to tell what it dreamed about.

> One impulse from a vernal wood,
> May teach you more of man,
> Of moral evil and of good,
> Than all the sages can.
>
> WORDSWORTH.

THE TREE THAT TRIED TO GROW

BY FRANCIS LEE

ONE time there was a seed that wished to be a
tree. It was fifty years ago, and more than fifty
— a hundred, perhaps.

But first there was a great bare granite rock in the
midst of the Wendell woods. Little by little, dust
from a squirrel's paw, as he sat upon it eating a nut;
fallen leaves, crumbling and rotting — and perhaps the decayed shell of the nut — made earth
enough in the hollows of the rock for some
mosses to grow; and for the tough little saxifrage
flowers, which seem to thrive on the poorest
fare, and look all the healthier, like very poor
children.

Then, one by one, the mosses and blossoms
withered, and turned to dust; until, after years,
and years, and years, there was earth enough to

make a bed for a little feathery birch seed which came flying along one day.

The sun shone softly through the forest trees; the summer rain pattered through the leaves upon it; and the seed felt wide awake and full of life. So it sent a little, pale-green stem up into the air, and a little white root down into the shallow bed of earth. But you would have been surprised to see how much the root found to feed upon in only a handful of dirt.

Yes, indeed! And it sucked and sucked away with its little hungry mouths, till the pale-green stem became a small brown tree, and the roots grew tough and hard.

So, after a great many years, there stood a tall tree as big around as your body, growing right upon a large rock, with its big roots striking into the ground on all sides of the rock, like a queer sort of wooden cage.

Now, I do not believe there was ever a boy in this world who tried as hard to grow into a wise, or a rich or a good man, as this birch seed did to grow into a tree, that did not become what he wished to be. And I don't think anybody who hears the story of the birch tree, growing in the woods of Wendell, need ever give up to any sort of difficulty in this way, and say: "I can't." Only try as hard as the tree did, and you can do everything.

HOW TO MAKE A WHISTLE

ANONYMOUS

First take a willow bough,
　　Smooth, and round, and dark;
And cut a little ring
　　Just through the outside bark.

Then tap and rap it gently,
　　With many a pat and pound,
To loosen up the bark,
　　So it may turn around.

Slip the bark off carefully,
　　So that it will not break,
And cut away the inside part,
　　And then a mouth-piece make.

Now put the bark all nicely back,
　　And in a single minute,
Just put it to your lips
　　And blow the whistle in it.

THE FOREST*

BY HENRY D. THOREAU

From *The Maine Woods*

Who shall describe the inexpressible tenderness and immortal life of the grim forest, where Nature,

*By permission of the publishers, Houghton, Mifflin & Co.

though it be mid-winter, is ever in her spring, where the moss-grown and decaying trees are not old, but seem to enjoy a perpetual youth; and blissful, innocent Nature, like a serene infant, is too happy to make a noise, except by a few tinkling, lisping birds and trickling rills?

LIFE'S FOREST TREES

BY ELLA WHEELER WILCOX

THE day grows brief; the afternoon is slanting
　　Down to the west; there is no time to waste.
If you have any seed of good for planting,
　　You must, you must make haste.

Not as of old do you enjoy earth's pleasures
　　(The only joys that last are those we give).
Across the grave you cannot take gains, treasures;
　　But good and kind deeds live.

I would not wait for any great achievement;
　　You may not live to reach that far-off goal.
Speak soothing words to some heart in bereavement—
　　Aid some up-struggling soul.

Teach some weak life to strive for independence;
　　Reach out a hand to some one in sore need.
Though it seem idle, yet in their descendants
　　May blossom this chance seed.

On each life path, like costly flowers faded
  And cast away, are pleasures that are dead;
Good deeds, like trees, whereunder, fed and shaded,
  Souls yet unborn may tread.

WOOD*

BY JULIA ROGERS

TREES grow, therefore wood is cheaper than metals. It is easily worked with tools into desired shapes and sizes. It is held securely by nails and by glue. It is practically permanent when protected by paint; under water or in the ground it outlasts metal. Its strength and lightness adapt it to various uses. Its lightness makes it easy to handle. It preserves the flavor of wines as no other material can do. It is a non-conductor of heat and electricity. Many woods are marked by patterns of infinite variety and beauty, whose very irregularities constitute an abiding charm. To this is added a fine blending of colors and a lustre when polished that give woods a place in the decorative arts that can be taken by no other substance.

THE HOLLY-TREE

BY ROBERT SOUTHEY

O READER! hast thou ever stood to see
  The Holly-tree?

----

* From " The Tree Book," Doubleday, Page & Co.

The eye that contemplates it will perceive
    Its glossy leaves,
Ordered by an intelligence so wise
As might confound the Atheist's sophistries.

Below, a circling fence, its leaves are seen,
    Wrinkled and keen;
No grazing cattle through their prickly round
    Can reach to wound;
But, as they grow where nothing is to fear,
Smooth and unarmed the pointless leaves appear.

I love to view these things with curious eyes,
    And moralize;
And in this wisdom of the Holly-tree
    Can emblem see
Wherewith, perchance, to make a pleasant rhyme,
One which may profit in the after-time.

Thus, though abroad perchance I might appear
    Harsh and austere,
To those who on my leisure would intrude
    Reserved and rude,
Gentle at home amid my friends I'd be,
Like the high leaves upon the Holly-tree.

And should my youth, as youth is apt I know,
    Somehow a harshness show,
All vain asperities I day by day
    Would wear away,

Till the smooth temper of my age should be
Like the high leaves upon the Holly-tree.

And as, when all the summer trees are seen
    So bright and green,
The Holly-leaves a sober hue display
    Less bright than they,
But when the bare and wintry woods we see,
What then so cheerful as the Holly-tree?

So serious should my youth appear among
    The thoughtless throng;
So would I seem, amid the young and gay,
    More grave than they,
That in my age as cheerful I might be
As the green winter of the Holly-tree.

A DISCOURSE ON TREES

BY HENRY WARD BEECHER

To the great tree-loving fraternity we belong. We love trees with universal and unfeigned love, and all things that do grow under them, or around them — "the whole leaf and root tribe." Not alone where they are in their glory, but in whatever state they are — in leaf, or ruined with frost, or powdered with snow, or crystal-sheathed in ice, or in severe outline stripped and bare against a November sky — we love them. Our heart warms at the sight of even a board or a log. A lumber yard is better than nothing. The smell of wood, at least, is there, the savory fragrance of resin, as sweet as myrrh and frankincense ever was to a Jew. If we can get nothing better, we love to read over the names of trees in a catalogue. Many an hour have we sat at night, when after exciting work, we needed to be quieted, and read nurserymen's catalogues, and London's Encyclopedias, and Arboretum, until the smell of the woods exhaled from the page, and the sound of leaves was in our ears, and sylvan glades opened to our eyes that would have made old Chaucer laugh and indite a rapturous rush of lines.

But how much more do we love trees in all their summer pomp and plenitude. Not for their names and affinities, not for their secret physiology and as material for science, not for any reason that we can give, except that when with them we are happy. The eye is full, the ear is full, the whole sense and all the tastes solaced, and our whole nature rejoices with that various and full happiness which one has when the soul is suspended in the midst of Beethoven's symphonies and is lifted hither and thither, as if blown by sweet sounds through the airy passage of a full heavenly dream.

Our first excursion in Lenox was one of saluta-tion to our notable trees. We had a nervous anxiety to see that the axe had not hewn, nor the lightning struck them; that no worm had gnawed at the root, or cattle at the trunk; that their branches were not broken, nor their leaves failing from drought. We found them all standing in their uprightness. They lifted up their heads toward heaven, and sent down to us from all their boughs a leafy whisper of recognition and affection. Blessed be the dew that cools their evening leaves, and the rains that quench their daily thirst! May the storm be as merciful to them when in winter it roars through their branches, as is a harper to his harp! Let the snow lie lightly on their boughs, and long hence be the summer that shall find no leaves to clothe these nobles of the pasture!

First in our regard, as it is in the whole nobility of trees, stands the white elm, no less esteemed because it is an American tree, known abroad only by importation, and never seen in all its magnificence, except in our own valleys. The old oaks of England are very excellent in their way, gnarled and rugged. The elm has strength as significant as they, and a grace, a royalty, that leaves the oak like a boor in comparison. Had the elm been an English tree, and had Chaucer seen and loved and sung it; had Shakespeare and every English poet hung some garlands upon it, it would have lifted up its head now, not only the noblest of all growing things, but enshrined in a thousand rich associations of history and literature.

Whoever sees a hawthorn or a sweetbrier (the eglantine) that his thoughts do not, like a bolt of light, burst through ranks of poets, and ranges of sparkling conceits which have been born since England had a written language, and of which the rose, the willow, the eglantine, the hawthorn, and scores of other vines or trees, have been the cause, as they are now and forevermore the suggestors and remembrancers?   Whoever looks upon an oak, and does not think of navies, of storms, of battles on the ocean, of the noble lyrics of the sea, of English glades, of the fugitive Charles, the tree-mounted monarch, of the Herne oak, of parks and forests, of Robin Hood and his merry men, Friar Tuck not excepted; of old baronial halls with mellow light streaming through diamond-shaped panes upon oaken floors, and of carved oaken wainscotings; And who that has ever traveled in English second-class, cushionless cars has not other and less genial remembrances of the enduring solidity of the impervious, unelastic oak?

One stalwart oak I have, and only one, yet discovered. On my west line is a fringe of forest, through which rushes, in spring, trickles in early summer, and dies out entirely in August, the issues of a noble spring from the near hillside. On the eastern edge of this belt of trees stands the monarchical oak, wide-branching on the east toward the open pasture and the free light, but on its western side lean and branchless from the pressure of neighboring trees; for trees, like men, cannot grow to the real nature that is in them when crowded by too much society. Both need to be touched on every side by sun and air, and by nothing else, if they are to be rounded out into full symmetry. Growing right up by its side, and through its branches is a long, wifely elm — beauty and grace imbosomed by strength. Their leaves come and go together, and all the summer long they mingle their rustling harmonies. Their roots pasture in the same soil, nor could either of them be hewn down without tearing away the branches and marring the beauty of the other. And a tree, when thoroughly disbranched, may, by time and care, regain its health again, but never its beauty.

Under this oak I love to sit and hear all the things which its leaves have to tell. No printed leaves have more treasures of history or of literature to those who know how to listen.   But, if clouds kindly shield us from the sun, we love as well to crouch down on the grass some thirty yards off and, amidst the fragrant smell of crushed herbs, to watch the fancies of the trees and clouds. The roguish winds will never be done teasing the leaves, that run away and come back, with nimble playfulness. Now and then a stronger puff dashes up the leaves, showing the downy under-surfaces that flash white all along the up-blown and tremulous forest edge.   Now the wind draws back his breath, and all the woods are still. Then some single leaf is tickled, and quivers all alone. I am sure there is no wind. The other leaves about it are still. Where it gets its motion I cannot tell, but there it goes fanning itself and restless among its sober fellows. By and by one or two others catch the impulse. The rest hold out a moment, but soon catching the contagious merriment, away goes the whole tree and all its neighbors, the leaves running in ripples all down the forest side. I expect almost to hear them laugh out loud. A stroke of wind upon the forest, indolently swelling and subsiding, is like a stroke upon a hive of bees, for sound; and like stirring a fire full of sparks for upspringing thoughts and ideal suggestions. The melodious whirl draws out a flittering swarm of sweet images that play before the eye like those evening troops of gauzy insects that hang in the air between you and the sun, and pipe their own music, and flit in airy rounds of mingled dance as if the whole errand of their lives was to swing in mazes of sweet music.

Different species of trees move their leaves very differently, so that one may sometimes tell by the motion of shadows on the ground, if he be too indolent to look up, under what kind of tree he is dozing. On the tulip-tree (which has the finest name that ever tree had, making the very pronouncing of its name almost like the utterance of a strain of music — *liriodendron tulipfera*) — on the tulip-tree, the aspen, and on all native poplars, the leaves are apparently Anglo-Saxon or Germanic, having an intense individualism. Each one moves to suit itself. Under the same wind one is trilling up and down, another is whirling, another slowly vibrating right and left, and others still, quieting themselves to sleep, as a mother gently pats her slumbering child; and each one intent upon a motion of its own. Sometimes other trees have single frisky leaves, but, usually, the oaks, maples beeches, have community of motion. They are all acting together, or all are alike still.

What is sweeter than a murmur of leaves, unless it be the musical gurgling of water that runs secretly and cuts under the roots of these trees, and makes little bubbling pools that laugh to see the drops stumble over the root and plump down into its bosom! In such nooks could trout lie. Unless ye would become mermaids, keep far from such places, all innocent grasshoppers, and all ebony crickets! Do not believe in appearances. You peer over and know an enemy lurks in that fairy pool. You can see every nook and corner of it, and it is as sweet a bathing-pool as ever was swam by long-legged grasshoppers. Over the root comes a butterfly with both sails a little drabbled, and quicker than light he is plucked down, leaving three or four bubbles behind him, fit emblems of a butterfly's life. There! did I not tell you? Now go away, all maiden crickets and grasshoppers! These fair surfaces, so pure, so crystalline, so surely safe, have a trout somewhere in them lying in wait for you!

But what if one sits between both kinds of music, leaves above and water below? What if birds are among the leaves, sending out random calls, far-piercing and sweet, as if they were lovers saying: "My dear, are you there?" If you are half reclining upon a cushion of fresh new moss, that swells up between the many-piled and twisted roots of a huge beech tree, and if you have been there half an hour without moving, and if you will still keep motionless; you may see what they who only walk through forests never see. . . .

Thus do you stand, noble elms! Lifted up so high are your topmost boughs, that no indolent birds care to seek you; and only those of nimble wings, and they with unwonted beat, that love exertion, and aspire to sing where none sing higher. Aspiration! so Heaven gives it pure as flames to the noble bosom. But debased with passion and selfishness it comes to be only Ambition!

It was in the presence of this pasture-elm, which we name the Queen, that we first felt to our very marrow, that we had indeed become owners of the soil. It was with a feeling of awe that we looked up into its face, and when I whispered to myself: "This is mine," there was a shrinking as if there were sacrilege in the very thought of *property* in such a creature of God as this cathedral-topped tree! Does a man bare his head in some old church? So did I, standing in the shadow of this regal tree, and looking up into that completed glory, at which three hundred years have been at work with noiseless fingers! What was I in its presence but a grasshopper? My heart said: "I may not call thee property, and that property mine! Thou belongest to the air. Thou art the child of summer. Thou art the mighty temple where birds praise God. Thou belongest to no man's hand, but to all men's eyes that do love beauty, and that have learned through beauty to behold God! Stand, then, in thine own beauty and grandeur! I shall be a lover and a protector, to keep drought from thy roots, and the axe from thy trunk."

For, remorseless men there are crawling yet upon the face of the earth, smitten blind and inwardly dead, whose only thought of a tree of ages is, that it is food for the axe and the saw! These are the wretches of whom the Scripture speaks: "*A man was famous according as he had lifted up axes upon the thick trees.*"

Thus famous, or rather infamous, was the last owner but one, before me, of this farm. Upon the crown of the hill, just where an artist would have planted them, had he wished to have them exactly in the right place, grew some two hundred stalwart and ancient maples, beeches, ashes, and oaks, a narrow belt-like forest, forming a screen from the northern and western winds in winter, and a harp of endless music for the summer. The wretched owner of this farm, tempted of the Devil, cut down the whole blessed band and brotherhood of trees, that he might fill his pocket with two pitiful dollars a cord for the wood! Well, his pocket was the best part of him. The iron furnaces have devoured my grove, and their huge stumps, that stood like gravestones, have been cleared away, that a grove may be planted in the same spot, for the next hundred years to nourish into the stature and glory of that which is gone.

In other places I find the memorials of many noble trees slain; here, a hemlock that carried up its eternal green a hundred feet into the winter air; there, a huge double-trunked chestnut, dear old grandfather of hundreds of children that have for generations clubbed its boughs, or shook its nut-laden top, and laughed and shouted as bushels of chestnuts rattled down. Now, the tree exists only in the form of looped-holed posts and weather-browned rails. I do hope the fellow got a sliver in his fingers every time he touched the hemlock plank, or let down the bars made of those chestnut rails!

To most people a grove is a grove, and all groves are alike. But no two groves are alike. There is as marked a difference between different forests as between different communities. A grove of pines without underbrush, carpeted with the fine-fingered russet leaves of the pine, and odorous of resinous gums, has scarcely a trace of likeness to a maple woods, either in the insects, the birds, the shrubs, the light and shade, or the sound of its leaves. If we lived in olden times among young mythologies, we should say that pines held the imprisoned spirits of naiads and water-nymphs, and that their sounds were of the water for whose lucid depths they always sighed. At any rate, the first pines must have grown on the seashore, and learned their first accents from the surf and the waves; and all their posterity have inherited the sound, and borne it inland to the mountains.

I like best a forest of mingled trees, ash, maple, oak, beech, hickory, and evergreens, with birches growing along the edges of the brook that carries itself through the roots and stones, toward the willows that grow in yonder meadow. It should be deep and sombre in some directions, running off into shadowy recesses and coverts beyond all footsteps. In such a wood there is endless variety. It will breathe as many voices to your fancy as might be brought from any organ beneath the pressure of some Handel's hands. By the way, Handel and Beethoven always remind me of forests. So do some poets, whose numbers are various as the infinity of vegetation, fine as the choicest cut leaves, strong and rugged in places as the unbarked trunk and gnarled roots at the ground's surface. Is there any other place, except the seaside, where hours are so short and moments so swift as in a forest? Where else, except in the rare communion of those friends much loved, do we awake from pleasure, whose calm flow is without a ripple, into surprise that whole hours are gone which we thought but just begun — blossomed and dropped, which we thought but just budding!

––––––

FOREIGN LANDS

BY ROBERT LOUIS STEVENSON

Up into the cherry-tree
Who should climb but little me?
I held the trunk with both my hands;
And looked abroad on foreign lands.

I saw the next-door garden lie,
Adorned with flowers, before my eye,
And many pleasant places more
That I had never seen before.

I saw the dimpling river pass
And be the sky's blue looking-glass;
And dusty roads go up and down,
And people tramping into town.

If I could find a higher tree,
Farther and farther I could see,
To where the grown-up river slips
Into the sea among the ships —

To where the roads on either hand
Lead onward into fairyland,
Where all the children dine at five,
And all the playthings are alive.

———

THE POPULAR POPLAR TREE

BY BLANCHE WILLIS HOWARD

WHEN the great wind sets things whirling,
    And rattles the window-panes,
And blows the dust in giants
    And dragons tossing their manes;
When the willows have waves like water,
    And children are shouting with glee;
When the pines are alive and the larches —
    Then hurrah for you and me,
In the tip o' the top o' the top o' the tip of the popu-
    lar poplar tree!

Don't talk about Jack and the Beanstalk —
    He did not climb half so high!
And Alice in all her travels
    Was never so near the sky!

Only the swallow, a-skimming
   The storm-cloud over the lea,
Knows how it feels to be flying —
   When the gusts come strong and free —
In the tip o' the top o' the top o' the tip of the popu-
   lar poplar tree!

THE BEECH TREE'S PETITION

BY THOMAS CAMPBELL

LEAVE this barren spot to me!
Spare, woodman, spare the beechen tree!
Though bush or floweret never grow
My dark, unwarming shade below;
Nor summer bud perfume the dew
Of rosy blush, or yellow hue!
Nor fruits of autumn, blossom-born,
My green and glossy leaves adorn;
Nor murmuring tribes from me derive
Th' ambrosial amber of the hive;
Yet leave this barren spot to me:
Spare, woodman, spare the beechen **tree!**

Thrice twenty summers I have seen
The sky grow bright, the forest green;
And many a wintry wind have stood
In bloomless, fruitless solitude,
Since childhood in my pleasant bower
First spent its sweet and sportive hour;

Since youthful lovers in my shade
Their vows of truth and rapture made;
And on my trunk's surviving frame
Carv'd many a long-forgotten name.
Oh! by the sighs of gentle sound,
First breathed upon this sacred ground;
By all that Love has whisper'd here,
Or beauty heard with ravish'd ear;
As Love's own altar honor me:
Spare, woodman, spare the beechen tree!

————

WOOD-SONG*

BY JOSEPHINE PRESTON PEABODY

LOVE must be a fearsome thing
    That can bind a maid
Glad of life as leaves in spring,
    Swift and unafraid.

I could find a heart to sing
    Death and darkness, praise or blame;
    But before that name,
Heedfully, oh, heedfully,
    Do I lock my breast;
I am silent as a tree,
    Guardful of the nest.

Ah, my passing Woodlander,
    Heard you any note?

* By permission of the publishers, Houghton, Mifflin & Co.

Would you find a leaf astir
  From a wilding throat?

Surely, all the paths defer
  Unto such a gentle quest.
  Would you take the nest?
Follow where the sun-motes are!
  Truly 'tis a sorrow
I must bid you fare so far;
  Speed you, and good-morrow!

THE WIND IN THE PINES

BY MADISON CAWEIN

WHEN winds go organing through the pines
  On hill and headland, darkly gleaming,
Meseems I hear sonorous lines
  Of Iliads that the woods are dreaming.

TO A MAPLE SEED*

BY LLOYD MIFFLIN

ART thou some wingéd Sprite, that, fluttering round,
Exhausted on the grass at last doth lie,
Or wayward Fay? Ah, weakling, by and by
Thyself shalt grow a giant, strong and sound,
When, like Antæus, thou dost touch the ground.

---

* Used by permission of the author.

O happy Seed!   It is not thine to die;
Thy wings bestow thine immortality,
And thou canst bridge the deep and dark profound.
I hear the ecstatic song the wild bird flings,
In future summers, from thy leafy head!
What hopes! what fears! what rapturous sufferings
What burning words of love will there be said!
What sobs — what tears! what passionate whisper-
    ings!
Under thy boughs, when I, alas! am dead.

FROM
SUNRISE*
BY SIDNEY LANIER

I HAVE waked, I have come, my beloved!   I might
    not abide:
I have come ere the dawn, O beloved, my live-oaks,
    to hide
    In your gospelling glooms — to be
As a lover in heaven, the marsh my marsh and the
    sea my sea.

Tell me, sweet burly-bark'd, man-bodied Tree
That mine arms in the dark are embracing, dost
    know
From what fount are these tears at thy feet which
    flow?

---

* From " The Poems of Sidney Lanier," copyright, 1884, 1891,
    by Mary D. Lanier; published by Charles Scribner's Sons.

They rise not from reason, but deeper, inconsequent
   deeps.
   Reason's not one that weeps.
   What logic of greeting lies
Betwixt dear over-beautiful trees and the rain of the
   eyes?

O cunning green leaves, little masters! like as ye
   gloss
All the dull-tissued dark with your luminous darks
   that emboss
 The vague blackness of night into pattern and
   plan,
   So
(But would I could know, but would I could know)
With your question embroid'ring the dark of the
   question of man —
So, with your silences purfling this silence of man.
While his cry to the dead for some knowledge is
   under the ban,
   Under the ban —
   So, ye have wrought me
Designs on the night of our knowledge — yea, ye
   have taught me,
   So,
That haply we know somewhat more than we know.

 Ye lisperers, whisperers, singers in storms,
 Ye consciences murmuring faiths under forms,
 Ye ministers meet for each passion that grieves,

Friendly, sisterly, sweetheart leaves,
Oh, rain me down from your darks that contain me
Wisdoms ye winnow from winds that pain me —
    Sift down tremors of sweet-within-sweet
    That advise me of more than they bring — repeat
Me the wood smell that swiftly but now brought
    breath
From the heaven-side bank of the river of death —
    Teach me the terms of silence —preach me
    The passion of patience — sift me — impeach me,
      And there, oh there,
As ye hang with your myriad palms upturned in
    the air,
      Pray me a myriad prayer.

VI

FLOWERS AND LEAVES OF GRASS

A HAPPY THOUGHT

OF HENRY WARD BEECHER'S

FLOWERS are the sweetest things that God ever made and forgot to put a soul into.

FLOWERS

BY JOHN MILTON

From *Lycidas*

YE VALLEYS low, where the mild whispers rise
Of shades and wanton winds and gushing brooks,
On whose fresh lap the swart star sparely looks,
Throw hither all your quaint enamel'd eyes,
That on the green turf suck the honey'd showers,
And purple all the ground with vernal flowers.
Bring the rathe primrose that forsaken dies,
The tufted crow-toe and pale jessamine,
The white pink and the pansy freak'd with jet,
The glowing violet,
The musk rose, and the well-attired woodbine,
With cowslips wan that hang the pensive head,
And every flower that sad embroidery wears;
Bid Amaranthus all his beauty shed,
And daffodillies fill their cups with tears,
To strew the laureate hearse where Lycid lies.

PLANTS AND FLOWERS

BY JOHN RUSKIN

WONDERFUL, in universal adaptation to man's need, God's daily preparation of the earth with beautiful means of life. First, a carpet, to make it soft for him; then a colored fantasy of embroidery thereon; then, tall spreading of foliage, to shade him from sun-heat, and shade also the fallen rain, that it may not dry quickly into the clouds, but stay to nourish the springs among the moss. Stout wood to bear this leafage; easily to be cut, yet tough and light, to make houses for him, or instruments; useless it had been if harder; useless if less fibrous; useless if less elastic.

Winter comes, and the shade of leafage falls away, to let the sun warm the earth; the strong boughs remain, breaking the strength of winter winds. The seeds, which are to prolong the race, innumerable according to the need, are made beautiful and palatable, varied into infinitude of appeal to the fancy of man, or provision for his service; cold juice or flowing spice, or balm, or incense, softening oil, preserving resin, medicine of febrifuge or lulling charm; and all these presented in forms of endless change.

SEEKING THE MAYFLOWER*

BY EDMUND CLARENCE STEDMAN

THE sweetest sound our whole year round —
  'Tis the first robin of the spring!
The song of the full orchard choir
  Is not so fine a thing.

Glad sights are common: Nature draws
  Her random pictures through the year,
But oft her music bids us long
  Remember those most dear.

To me, when in the sudden spring
  I hear the earliest robin's lay,
With the first trill there comes again
  One picture of the May.

The veil is parted wide, and lo,
  A moment though my eyelids close,
Once more I see that wooded hill
  Where the arbutus grows.

I see the village dryad kneel,
  Trailing her slender fingers through
The knotted tendrils, as she lifts
  Their pink, pale flowers to view.

* By permission of the publishers, Houghton, Mifflin & Co.

Once more I dare to stoop beside
　　The dove-eyed beauty of my choice,
And long to touch her careless hair,
　　And think how dear her voice.

My eager, wandering hands assist
　　With fragrant blooms her lap to fill,
And half by chance they meet her own,
　　Half by our young hearts' will.

Till, at the last, those blossoms won —
　　Like her, so pure, so sweet, so shy —
Upon the gray and lichened rocks
　　Close at her feet I lie.

Fresh blows the breeze through hemlock trees,
　　The fields are edged with green below;
And naught but youth and hope and love
　　We know or care to know!

Hark! from the moss-clung apple-bough,
　　Beyond the tumbled wall, there broke
That gurgling music of the May —
　　'Twas the first robin spoke!

I heard it, ay, and heard it not —
　　For little then my glad heart wist
What toil and time should come to pass,
　　And what delight be missed;

Nor thought thereafter, year by year,
  Hearing that fresh yet olden song,
To yearn for unreturning joys
  That with its joy belong.

———

THE STORY OF THE HYACINTH

ANONYMOUS

HYACINTH was a beautiful youth beloved by Apollo. He was playing one day at discus-throwing with the god, when Zephyrus, the West Wind, enraged at Hyacinthus for preferring Apollo to himself, caused one of the discuses to rebound and strike him in the face. Apollo, in despair, seeing that he was unable to save his life, changed him into the flower which bears his name, on whose petals Grecian fancy traced *ai, ai*, the notes of grief.

———

CHILDREN AND FLOWERS

BY AMANDA B. HARRIS

From *Wild Flower Papers*

WHAT do these children do who never have a chance to gather wild flowers — the flowers that bloom so lavishly; more than enough for everybody, in the dear country-places?

Never to have been where violets grow, or arbutus,

or down in those lovely woods among the beds of linnæa! Never to have found the spring-beauty and the wood-sorrel, and the dog's-tooth violet, and Jack-in-the-pulpit! Never to have seen banks of scarlet columbine, and a whole milky-way of the silvery miterwort! Never to have come home from the pasture with lady's slippers and red lilies; or been on the meadows in cowslip time, or by the pond when the lilies were open! Never to have had all the goldenrod and asters one wanted!

It seems as if a child had not had his rightful share in this world when he has been limited to some pent-up court or narrow street. Every child is born with a love for flowers. Yet many a little one must be satisfied with the dandelion that comes up in the backyard, which the eager fingers reach for as a miser would for gold.

Every generous boy and girl who has been used to having wild flowers enough must have often longed to share them with those who had none; to send them by the barrel full; to load down express wagons with daisies and lilies (oh, so many there are on the green meadows in midsummer!) and have them distributed all along those city byways, and in the hospitals where sick children are lying in pain. It would be like opening the doors and letting the country in; for they would carry with them the dew of the meadows, and the woodsy smells. You could almost seem to hear the cow-bells tinkle, the singing of birds, the gurgling of happy brooks, murmur of bees, and lowing of cattle, and the whistle of the farm boys at their work; for they all belong together.

THE VIOLET UNDER THE SNOW

BY RACHEL CAPEN SCHAUFFLER

To THEE I would bring
  Through all thy dead winter
Th' perfume of Spring.

With thee I would share
  The gold in the burden
Brave hearts have to bear.

Art happy to see,
  O Child of the Purple;
A Brother in me?

THE PRIMROSES*

BY W. GRAHAM ROBERTSON

WHAT has happened in the night?
  All the stars are fallen down!
Won't they set the earth a-light?
  — Earth so old and brown.
We can pick them as we pass,
  Scattered shining on the grass.

---

* Published by the John Lane Company, New York and London.

Here is Venus, here is Mars,
   Here's a bunch of Pleiades.
(Did you ever know that stars
   Smelt as sweet as these?)
Here's a golden girdle, too;
What will poor Orion do?

Let us, from some hidden nook,
   Watch for Folk Beyond the Moon.
Don't you think they'll come to look
   For the truants soon?
Wait until the sun has set,
For they won't have missed them yet.

A SAYING OF LINNÆUS*

BY JOHN FISKE

From *Through Nature to God*

I OFTEN think, when working over my plants, of what Linnæus once said of the unfolding of a blossom: "I saw God in His glory passing near me, and bowed my head in worship." The scientific aspect of the same thought has been put into words by Tennyson:

Flower in the crannied wall,
I pluck you out of the crannies;
Hold you here, root and all, in my hand,
Little flower — but if I could understand
What you are, root and all, and all in all,
I should know what God and man is.

---

* By permission of the publishers, Houghton, Mifflin & Co.

No deeper thought was ever uttered by poet. For in this world of plants, which with its magician, chlorophyll, conjuring with sunbeams, is ceaselessly at work bringing life out of death — and in this quiet vegetable world we may find the elementary principles of all life in almost visible operation.

————

OF GARDENS

BY FRANCIS BACON

AND because the breath of flowers is far sweeter in the air, where it comes and goes, like the warbling of music, than in the hand, therefore nothing is more for that delight, than to know what be the flowers and plants that do best perfume the air. That which above all others yields the sweetest smell in the air is the violet; especially the white double violet, which comes twice a year, about the middle of April, and about Bartholomew-tide. Next to that is the musk rose; then the strawberry leaves dying, with a most excellent cordial smell; then the flower of the vines — it is a little dust, like the dust of a bent, which grows upon the cluster, in the first coming forth; then sweetbrier; then wallflowers, which are very delightful, to be set under a parlor, or lower chamber window; then pinks and gillyflowers, especially the matted pink and clove gillyflower; then the flowers of the lime tree; then the

honeysuckles, so they be somewhat afar off. Of
bean-flowers, I speak not, because they are field
flowers; but those which perfume the air most
delightfully, not passed by as the rest, but being
trodden upon and crushed, are three; that is, burnet,
wild thyme, and water mints. Therefore you are to
set whole alleys of them, to have the pleasure when you
walk or tread.

I KNOW A BANK

BY WILLIAM SHAKESPEARE

I KNOW a bank whereon the wild-thyme blows,
Where oxlips, and the nodding violet grows;
Quite over-canopied with lush woodbine,
With sweet musk-roses, and with eglantine:
There sleeps Titania, some time of the night,
Lull'd in these flowers with dances and delight;
And there the snake throws her enamel'd skin,
Weed wide enough to wrap a fairy in.

LEAVES OF GRASS*

BY WALT WHITMAN

A CHILD said, What is the grass? fetching it to me
  with full hands;
How could I answer the child? I do not know what
  it is any more than he.

* From " Leaves of Grass," etc., published by David McKay,
Philadelphia, Pa.

I guess it must be the flag of my disposition, out of
    hopeful green stuff woven.
Or I guess it is the handkerchief of the Lord,
A scented gift and remembrancer designedly
    dropped,
Bearing the owner's name someway in the corners,
    that we may see and remark, and say Whose?
Or I guess the grass is itself a child, the produced
    babe of the vegetation.
Or I guess it is a uniform hieroglyphic,
And it means, Sprouting alike in broad zones and
    narrow zones,
Growing among black folks as among white,
Kanuck, Tuckahoe, Congressman, Cuff, I give them
    the same, I receive them the same.
And now it seems to me the beautiful uncut hair of
    graves.
Tenderly will I use you, curling grass,
It may be you transpire from the breasts of young men,
It may be if I had known them I would have loved
    them,
It may be you are from old people, or from offspring
    taken soon out of their mothers' laps,
And here you are the mothers' laps.
This grass is very dark to be from the white heads
    of old mothers,
Darker than the colorless beards of old men,
Dark to come from under the faint red roofs of mouths.
Oh, I perceive after all so many uttering tongues,

And I perceive they do not come from the roofs of
mouths for nothing.

I wish I could translate the hints about the dead
young men and women,

And the hints about old men and mothers, and the
offspring taken soon out of their laps.

What do you think has become of the young and old
men?

And what do you think has become of the women
and children?

They are alive and well somewhere, the smallest
sprout shows there is really no death,

And if ever there was it led forward life, and does not
wait at the end to arrest it,

And ceased the moment life appeared.

All goes onward and outward, nothing collapses,

And to die is different from what any one supposed,
and luckier.

. . . .

I know I am deathless,

I know this orbit of mine cannot be swept by a
carpenter's compass,

I know I shall not pass like a child's carlacue cut with
a burnt stick at night.

. . . .

One world is away and by far the largest to me, and
that is myself,

And whether I come to my own to-day or in ten
thousand or ten million years,

I can cheerfully take it now, or with equal cheerful-
　　ness I can wait.
My foothold is tenoned and mortised in granite,
I laugh at what you call dissolution,
And I know the amplitude of time.

THE STORY OF NARCISSUS

ANONYMOUS

NARCISSUS was a beautiful youth, who, seeing his
image reflected in a fountain, became so enamored
of it that he pined away and was finally changed into
the flower that bears his name. Poetic legends
regard this as a just punishment for his hard-hearted-
ness to Echo, and other wood-nymphs and maidens,
who had loved him devotedly.

The narcissus loves the borders of streams, and is
admirably personified in the story, for bending on its
fragile stem it seems to be always seeking to see its
own image reflected in the waters.

FROM

A WILD STRAWBERRY*

BY HENRY VAN DYKE

FOR my own part, I approve of garden flowers
because they are so orderly and so certain; but wild

---

* From " Fisherman's Luck," copyright, 1899, 1905, by Charles
Scribner's Sons.

flowers I love, just because there is so much chance about them. Nature is all in favor of certainty in great laws and of uncertainty in small events. You cannot appoint the day and the place for her flower shows. If you happen to drop in at the right moment she will give you a free admission. But even then it seems as if the table of beauty had been spread for the joy of a higher visitor, and in obedience to secret orders which you have not heard.

FLOWERS*

BY H. W. LONGFELLOW

SPAKE full well, in language quaint and olden,
  One who dwelleth by the castled Rhine,
When he called the flowers, so blue and golden,
  Stars, that in earth's firmament do shine.

Stars they are, wherein we read our history,
  As astrologers and seers of old;
Yet not wrapped about with awful mystery,
  Like the burning stars which they behold.

Wondrous truths, and manifold as wondrous,
  God hath written in those stars above;
But not less in the bright flowerets under us
  Stands the revelation of his love.

* By permission of the publishers, Houghton, Mifflin & Co.

Bright and glorious is that revelation,
  Written all over this great world of ours,
Making evident our own creation
  In these stars of earth, these golden flowers.

And the Poet, faithful and far-seeing,
  Sees, alike in stars and flowers, a part
Of the self-same, universal being
  Which is throbbing in his brain and heart.

Gorgeous flowerets in the sunlight shining,
  Blossoms flaunting in the eye of day,
Tremulous leaves with soft and silver lining,
  Buds that open only to decay,

Brilliant hopes all woven in gorgeous tissues,
  Flaunting gayly in the golden light;
Large desires, with most uncertain issues,
  Tender wishes, blossoming at night.

Those in flowers and men are more than seeming;
  Workings are they of the self-same powers
Which the Poet, in no idle dreaming,
  Seeth in himself and in the flowers.

Everywhere about us are they glowing —
  Some like stars, to tell us Spring is born;
Others, their blue eyes with tears o'erflowing,
  Stand like Ruth amid the golden corn.

Not alone in Spring's armorial bearing,
    And in Summer's green-emblazoned field,
But in arms of brave old Autumn's wearing,
    In the center of his brazen shield.

Not alone in meadows and green alleys,
    On the mountain-top, and by the brink
Of sequestered pools in woodland valleys,
    Where the slaves of Nature stoop to drink.

Not alone in her vast dome of glory,
    Not on graves of bird and beast alone,
But in old cathedrals, high and hoary,
    On the tombs of heroes, carved in stone;

In the cottage of the rudest peasant,
    In ancestral homes, whose crumbling towers,
Speaking of the Past unto the Present,
    Tell us of the ancient Games of Flowers;

In all places, then, and in all seasons,
    Flowers expand their light and soul-like wings,
Teaching us, by most persuasive reasons,
    How akin they are to human things.

And with child-like, credulous affection
    We behold their tender buds expand —
Emblems of our own great resurrection,
    Emblems of the bright and better land.

DAFFODILS

DAFFODILS

BY WILLIAM WORDSWORTH

I WANDERED lonely as a cloud
   That floats on high o'er vales and hills,
When all at once I saw a crowd,
   A host, of golden daffodils;
Beside the lake, beneath the trees,
Fluttering and dancing in the breeze.

Continuous as the stars that shine
   And twinkle on the Milky Way,
They stretched in never-ending line
   Along the margin of a bay:
Ten thousand saw I at a glance,
Tossing their heads in sprightly dance.

The waves beside them danced, but they
   Outdid the sparkling waves in glee:
A poet could not but be gay,
   In such a jocund company:
I gazed — and gazed — but little thought
What wealth the show to me had brought.

For oft, when on my couch I lie
   In vacant or in pensive mood,
They flash upon that inward eye
   Which is the bliss of solitude;
And then my heart with pleasure fills,
And dances with the daffodils.

THE WATER-LILY*

BY JOHN BANISTER TABB

WHENCE, O fragrant form of light,
Hast thou drifted through the night,
Swanlike, to a leafy nest,
On the restless waves, at rest?

Art thou from the snowy zone
Of a mountain-summit blown,
Or the blossom of a dream,
Fashioned in the foamy stream?

Nay — methinks the maiden moon,
When the daylight came too soon,
Fleeting from her bath to hide,
Left her garment in the tide.

TO A MOUNTAIN DAISY

BY ROBERT BURNS

WEE, modest, crimson-tippèd flow'r,
Thou's met me in an evil hour;
For I maun crush amang the stoure
    Thy slender stem;
To spare thee now is past my pow'r,
    Thou bonnie gem.

----

* By permission of the publishers, Houghton, Mifflin & Co.

Alas! it's no thy neebor sweet,
The bonnie lark, companion meet,
Bending thee 'mang the dewy weet,
  Wi' spreckled breast!
When upward-springing, blithe, to greet
  The purpling east.

Cauld blew the bitter-biting north
Upon thy early, humble birth;
Yet cheerfully thou glinted forth
  Amid the storm,
Scarce rear'd above the parent earth
  Thy tender form.

The flaunting flow'rs our gardens yield,
High shelt'ring woods and wa's maun shield,
But thou, beneath the random bield
  O' clod or stane,
Adorns the histie stibble-field
  Unseen, alane.

There, in thy scanty mantle clad,
Thy snawie bosom sunward spread,
Thou lifts thy unassuming head
  In humble guise;
But now the share uptears thy bed,
  And low thou lies!

Such is the fate of simple Bard,
On Life's rough ocean luckless starr'd!

Unskilful he to note the card
   Of prudent lore,
Till billows rage, and gales blow hard,
   And whelm him o'er!

Such fate to suffering Worth is given,
Who long with wants and woes has striv'n,
By human pride or cunning driv'n
   To mis'ry's brink;
Till, wrench'd of ev'ry stay but Heav'n,
   He, ruin'd, sink!

E'en thou who mourn'st the Daisy's fate,
That fate is thine — no distant date;
Stern Ruin's plowshare drives, elate,
   Full on thy bloom,
Till crush'd beneath the furrow's weight
   Shall be thy doom!

OLD FASHIONED FLOWERS*

BY MAURICE MAETERLINCK

THIS morning, when I went to look at my flowers, surrounded by their white fence, which protects them against the good cattle grazing in the field beyond, I saw again in my mind all that blossoms in the woods, the fields, the gardens, the orangeries, and the greenhouses, and I thought of

* Used by permission of M. Maeterlinck and Dodd, Mead & Co.

all that we owe to the world of marvels which the bees visit.

Can we conceive what humanity would be if it did not know the flowers? If these did not exist, if they had all been hidden from our gaze, as are probably a thousand no less fairy sights that are all around us, but invisible to our eyes, would our character, our faculties, our sense of the beautiful, our aptitude for happiness, be quite the same? We should, it is true, in nature have other splendid manifestations of luxury, exuberance, and grace; other dazzling efforts of the superfluous forces: the sun, the stars, the varied lights of the moon, the azure and the ocean, the dawns and twilights, the mountain, the plain, the forest and the rivers, the light and the trees, and lastly, nearer to us, birds, precious stones and woman. These are the ornaments of our planet. Yet but for the last three, which belong to the same smile of nature, how grave, austere, almost sad, would be the education of our eye without the softness which the flowers give! Suppose for a moment that our globe knew them not: a great region, the most enchanted in the joys of our psychology, would be destroyed, or rather would not be discovered. All of a delightful sense would sleep for ever at the bottom of our harder and more desert hearts and in our imagination stripped of worshipful images. The infinite world of colors and shades would have been but incompletely revealed to us by a few rents in the sky. The miraculous harmonies of light at play, ceaselessly inventing new gaieties, reveling in itself, would be unknown to us; for the flowers first broke up the prism and made the most subtle portion of our sight. And the magic garden of perfumes — who would have opened its gate to us? A few grasses, a few gums, a few fruits, the breath of the dawn. The smell of the night and the sea, would have told us that beyond our eyes and ears there existed a shut paradise where the air which we breathe changes into delights for which we could have found no name. Consider also all that the voice of human happiness would lack! One of the blessed heights of our soul would be almost dumb, if the flowers had not, since centuries, fed with their beauty the language which we speak and the thoughts that endeavor to crystallize the most precious hours of life. The whole vocabulary, all the impressions of love, are impregnate with their breath, nourished with their smile. When we love, all the flowers that we have seen and smelt seem to hasten within us to people with their known charms the consciousness of a sentiment whose happiness, but for them, would have no more form than the horizons of the sea or sky. They have accumulated within us, since our childhood, and even before it, in the soul of our fathers, an immense treasure, the nearest to our joys, upon which we draw each time that we wish to make more real the clement minutes of our life. They have created and spread in our world of sentiment the fragrant atmosphere in which love delights.

VIOLETS*

BY LUCY LARCOM

THEY neither toil nor spin;
   And yet their robes have won
A splendor never seen within
   The courts of Solomon.

Tints that the cloud-rifts hold,
   And rainbow-gossamer,
The violet's tender form enfold;
   No queen is draped like her.

All heaven and earth and sea
   Have wrought with subtlest power,
That clothed in purple she might be —
   This little fading flower.

We, who must toil and spin,
   What clothing shall we wear?
The glorious raiment we shall win,
   Life shapes us, everywhere.

God's inner heaven hath sun,
   And rain, and space of sky,
Wherethrough for us his spindles run,
   His mighty shuttles fly.

---

* By permission of the publishers, Houghton, Mifflin & Co.

His seamless vesture white
　He wraps our spirits in;
He weaves his finest webs of light
　For us, who toil and spin.

———

EPIGRAM*

BY ROBERT HAVEN SCHAUFFLER

(*With a handful of Plymouth Mayflowers*)

THE *Mayflower* once filled this shore
　With seekers after truth and duty;
And now, each April, fills it o'er
　With seekers after hidden beauty.

Would it had taught the Fathers why
Truth without beauty's half a lie;
　And would it might to us express
　The beauty of their holiness.

———

THE DAISY'S SONG
(*A Fragment*)

BY JOHN KEATS

THE sun, with his great eye,
Sees not as much as I;
　And the moon, all silver-proud,
　Might as well be in a cloud.

───

* By permission of The Century Co.

And O the spring — the spring!
I lead the life of a king!
Couch'd in the teeming grass,
I spy each pretty lass.

I look where no one dares,
And I stare where no one stares,
And when the night is nigh
Lambs bleat my lullaby.

THE RHODORA*

(*On Being asked, Whence is the Flower?*)

BY RALPH WALDO EMERSON

In May, when sea-winds pierced our solitudes,
I found the fresh Rhodora in the woods,
Spreading its leafless blooms in a damp nook,
To please the desert and the sluggish brook.
The purple petals, fallen in the pool,
Made the black water with their beauty gay;
Here might the redbird come, his plumes to cool,
And court the flower that cheapens his array.
Rhodora! if the sages ask thee why
This charm is wasted on the earth and sky,
Tell them, dear, that if eyes were made for
    seeing,

----

*By permission of the publishers, Houghton, Mifflin & Co.

Then Beauty is its own excuse for being:*
Why thou wert there, O rival of the rose!
I never thought to ask, I never knew:
But, in my simple ignorance, suppose
The self-same Power that brought me there brought
    you.

———

THE FIRST DANDELION

BY WALT WHITMAN

SIMPLE and fresh and fair from winter's close
    emerging,
As if no artifice of fashion, business, politics, had
    ever been,
Forth from its sunny nook of shelter'd grass —
    innocent, golden, calm as the dawn,
The spring's first dandelion shows its trustful face.

———

SWEET PEAS

BY JOHN KEATS

HERE are sweet peas, on tiptoe for a flight:
With wings of gentle flush o'er delicate white,
And taper fingers catching at all things,

———

* Compare the chapter on " Beauty," in Emerson's " Nature."
" This element (Beauty) I call an ultimate end. No reason can
be asked or given why the soul seeks beauty. Beauty, in its largest
and profoundest sense, is one expression for the universe. . . .
The ancient Greeks called the world Beauty."

To bind them all about with tiny rings.
Linger awhile upon some bending planks
That lean against a streamlet's rushy banks,
And watch intently Nature's gentle doings:
They will be found softer than ringdove's cooings.
How silent comes the water round that bend!
Not the minutest whisper does it send
To the o'erhanging sallows: blades of grass
Slowly across the chequer'd shadows pass.

THE STORY OF THE SUNFLOWER

ANONYMOUS

CLYTIE was a beautiful water-nymph in love with Apollo. But, alas! he did not love her. So she pined away, sitting all day on the cold, hard ground, with her unbound tresses streaming over her shoulders. Nine days she sat and tasted neither food nor drink, her own tears and the chilly dew her only food. She gazed on the sun when he rose, and as he passed through his daily course to his setting, she saw no other object, her face turned constantly to him. At last, they say, her limbs rooted to the ground, her face became a sunflower, which turns on its stem so as always to face the sun throughout its daily course; for it retains to that extent the feeling of the nymph from whom it sprang.

FLOWERS

BY WILLIAM SHAKESPEARE

               O PROSERPINA,
For the flowers now, that frighted, thou let'st fall
From Dis's wagon! daffodils,
That come before the swallow dares, and take
The winds of March with beauty; violets dim,
But sweeter than the lids of Juno's eyes,
Or Cytherea's breath; pale primroses,
That die unmarried, ere they can behold
Bright Phœbus in his strength, a malady
Most incident to maids; bold ox-lips, and
The crown-imperial; lilies of all kinds.
The flower-de-luce being one! O, these I lack,
To make you garlands of; and my sweet friend,
To strew him o'er and o'er!

A PITCHER OF MIGNONETTE

BY HENRY CUYLER BUNNER

A PITCHER of mignonette
   In a tenement's highest casement —
Queer sort of flower-pot — yet
That pitcher of mignonette
Is a garden in heaven set,
   To the little sick child in the basement —
The pitcher of mignonette,
   In the tenement's highest casement.

WILD FLOWERS

BY RICHARD JEFFERIES

From *The Open Air*

A FIR tree is not a flower, and yet it is associated in my mind with primroses. There was a narrow lane leading into a wood, where I used to go almost every day in the early months of the year, and at one corner it was overlooked by three spruce firs. The rugged lane there began to ascend the hill, and I paused a moment to look back. Immediately the high fir trees guided the eye upwards, and from their tops to the deep azure of the March sky over, but a step from the tree to the heavens. So it has ever been to me, by day or by night, summer or winter; beneath trees the heart feels nearer to that depth of life the far sky means. The rest of spirit found only in beauty, ideal and pure, comes there because the distance seems within touch of thought. To the heaven thought can reach lifted by the strong arms of the oak, carried up by the ascent of the flame-shaped fir. Round the spruce top the blue was deepened, concentrated by the fixed point, the memory of that spot, as it were, of the sky is still fresh — I can see it distinctly — still beautiful and full of meaning. It is painted in bright color in my mind, color thrice laid, and indelible; as one passes a shrine and bows the head to the Madonna, so I recall the picture and stoop in spirit to the aspiration it yet arouses. For there is no saint like the sky, sunlight shining from its face.

. . . .

Before I had any conscious thought it was a delight to me to find wild flowers, just to see them. It was a pleasure to gather them and to take them home; a pleasure to show them to others — to keep them as long as they would live, to decorate the room with them, to arrange them carelessly with grasses, green sprays, tree-bloom — large branches of chestnut snapped off, and set by a picture per-haps. Without conscious thought of seasons and the advancing hours to light on the white wild violet, the meadow orchis, the blue veronica, the blue meadow cranesbill; feeling the warmth and delight of the increasing sun-rays, but not recognizing whence or why it was joy. All the world is young to a boy, and thought has not entered into it; even the old men with gray hair do not seem old; different but not aged, the idea of age has not been mastered. A boy has to frown and study, and then does not grasp what long years mean. The various hues of the petals pleased without any knowledge of color-contrasts, no note even of color except that it was bright, and the mind was made happy without con-sideration of those ideals and hopes afterwards associated with the azure sky above the fir trees. A fresh footpath, a fresh flower, a fresh delight.

The reeds, the grasses, the rushes — unknown
and new things at every step — something always to
find; no barren spot anywhere, or sameness. Every
day the grass painted anew, and its green seen for the
first time; not the old green, but a novel hue and
spectacle, like the first view of the sea.

If we had never before looked upon the earth, but
suddenly came to it man or woman grown, set down
in the midst of a summer mead, would it not seem
to us a radiant vision? The hues, the shapes, the
song and life of birds, above all the sunlight, the
breath of heaven, resting on it; the mind would be
filled with its glory, unable to grasp it, hardly believing that such things could be mere matter and no
more. Like a dream of some spirit-land it would
appear, scarce fit to be touched lest it should fall to
pieces, too beautiful to be long watched lest it should
fade away. So it seemed to me as a boy, sweet and
new like this each morning; and even now, after
the years that have passed, and the lines they have
worn in the forehead, the summer mead shines as
bright and fresh as when my foot first touched the
grass. It has another meaning now; the sunshine
and the flowers speak differently, for a heart that
has once known sorrow reads behind the page, and
sees sadness in joy. But the freshness is still there,
the dew washes the colors before dawn. Uncon-
scious happiness in finding wild flowers — uncon-
scious and unquestioning, and therefore unbounded.

TO THE DANDELION
(*Extract*)
BY JAMES RUSSELL LOWELL

DEAR common flower, that grow'st beside the way,
  Fringing the dusty road with harmless gold,
First pledge of blithesome May,
  Which children pluck, and, full of pride uphold,
High-hearted buccaneers, o'erjoyed that they
  An Eldorado in the grass have found,
  Which not the rich earth's ample round
May match in wealth, thou art more dear to me
Than all the prouder summer-blooms may be.

―――

THE DANDELIONS
BY HELEN GRAY CONE

UPON a showery night and still,
  Without a sound of warning,
A trooper band surprised the hill,
  And held it in the morning.
We were not waked by bugle-notes,
  No cheer our dreams invaded,
And yet, at dawn, their yellow coats
  On the green slopes paraded.

We careless folk the deed forgot;
  Till one day, idly walking,

We marked upon the self-same spot
   A crowd of veterans talking.
They shook their trembling heads and gray
   With pride and noiseless laughter;
When, well-a-day! they blew away,
   And ne'er were heard of after!

———

TO A WIND FLOWER

BY MADISON CAWEIN

TEACH me the secret of thy loveliness,
   That, being made wise, I may aspire to be
As beautiful in thought, and so express
   Immortal truths to earth's mortality;
Though to my soul ability be less
   Than 'tis to thee, O sweet anemone.

Teach me the secret of thy innocence,
   That in simplicity I may grow wise,
Asking from Art no other recompense
   Than the approval of her own just eyes;
So may I rise to some fair eminence,
   Though less than thine, O cousin of the skies.

Teach me these things, through whose high knowl-
     edge, I —
   When Death hath poured oblivion through my
     veins,

And brought me home, as all are brought, to lie
  In that vast house, common to serfs and Thanes —
I shall not die, I shall not utterly die,
  For beauty born of beauty — *that remains.*

———

TO A WITHERED ROSE

BY JOHN KENDRICK BANGS

THY span of life was all too short —
  A week or two at best —
From budding-time, through blossoming,
  To withering and rest.

Yet compensation hast thou — aye —
  For all thy little woes;
For was it not thy happy lot
  To live and die a rose?

———

MARIGOLDS

BY JOHN KEATS

OPEN afresh your round of starry folds,
Ye ardent marigolds!
Dry up the moisture of your golden lids,
For great Appollo bids
That in these days your praises shall be sung

On many harps, which he has lately strung;
And then again your dewiness he kisses —
Tell him I have you in my world of blisses:
So haply when I rove in some far vale,
His mighty voice may come upon the gale.

A HOLLYHOCK

BY FRANK DEMPSTER SHERMAN

SERAGLIO of the Sultan Bee!
    I listen at the waxen door,
And hear the zithern's melody
    And sound of dancing on the floor.

WITH A SPRAY OF APPLE BLOSSOMS

BY WALTER LEARNED

THE promise of these fragrant flowers,
    The fruit that 'neath these blossoms lies
Once hung, they say, in Eden's bowers,
    And tempted Eve in Paradise.

O fairest daughter of Eve's blood,
    Lest her misprision thine should be,
I've nipped temptation in the bud
    And send this snowy spray to thee.

FOUR-LEAF CLOVER

BY ELLA HIGGINSON

I KNOW a place where the sun is like gold,
  And the cherry blooms burst with snow,
And down underneath is the loveliest nook,
  Where the four-leaf clovers grow.

One leaf is for hope, and one is for faith,
  And one is for love, you know,
And God put another one in for luck —
  If you search you will find where they grow.

But you must have hope, and you must have faith,
  You must love and be strong — and so —
If you work, if you wait, you will find the place
  Where the four-leaf clovers grow.

————

THE GRASS

BY EMILY DICKINSON

THE grass so little has to do —
  A spear of simple green,
With only butterflies to brood,
  And bees to entertain,

And stir all day to pretty tunes
  The breezes fetch along,

And hold the sunshine in its lap,
  And bow to everything;

And thread the dews all night, like pearls,
  And make itself so fine —
A duchess were too common
  For such a noticing.

And even when it dies, to pass
  In odors so divine —
As lowly spices gone to sleep,
  Or amulets of pine.

And then to dwell in sovereign barns,
  And dream the days away —
The grass so little has to do,
  I wish I were the hay!

———

GREEN THINGS GROWING

BY DINAH MARIA MULOCK

OH, THE green things growing, the green things
    growing,
The faint sweet smell of the green things growing!
I should like to live, whether I smile or grieve,
Just to watch the happy life of my green things
    growing.

Oh, the fluttering and the pattering of those green
    things growing!

How they talk each to each, when none of us are
    knowing;
In the wonderful white of the weird moonlight,
Or the dim dreamy dawn when the cocks are crowing.

I love, I love them so — my green things growing!
And I think that they love me, without false showing;
For by many a tender touch, they comfort me so
    much,
With the soft mute comfort of green things growing.

VII
CONSERVATION

DECLARATION OF PRINCIPLES

BY THE CONFERENCE ON THE CONSERVATION OF NATURAL RESOURCES, WHITE HOUSE, MAY 13, 1908

WE, THE governors of the states and territories of the United States of America in conference assembled, do hereby declare the conviction that the great prosperity of our country rests upon the abundant resources of the land chosen by our forefathers for their homes, and where they laid the foundation of this great nation.

We look upon these resources as a heritage to be made use of in establishing and promoting the comfort, prosperity, and happiness of the American people, but not to be wasted, deteriorated, or needlessly destroyed.

We agree that our country's future is involved in this; that the great natural resources supply the material basis upon which our civilization must continue to depend, and upon which the perpetuity of the nation itself rests.

We agree, in the light of the facts brought to our knowledge and from information received from sources which we cannot doubt, that this material basis is threatened with exhaustion. Even as each succeeding generation from the birth of the nation has performed its part in promoting the progress and development of the Republic, so do we in this generation recognize it as a high duty to perform our part; and this duty in large degree lies in the adoption of measures for the conservation of the natural wealth of the country.

We declare our firm conviction that this conservation of our natural resources is a subject of transcendent importance which should engage unremittingly the attention of the nation, the states, and the people in earnest coöperation. These natural resources include the land on which we live and which yields our food; the living waters which fertilize the soil, supply power, and form great avenues of commerce; the forests which yield the materials for our homes, prevent erosion of the soil, and conserve the navigation and other uses of the streams; and the minerals which form the basis of our industrial life, and supply us with heat, light, and power.

We agree that the land should be so used that erosion and soil wash shall cease; and that there should be reclamation of arid and semi-arid regions by means of irrigation, and of swamp and overflowed regions by means of drainage; that the waters should be so conserved and used as to promote navigation, to enable the arid regions to be reclaimed by irrigation, and to develop power in the interests of the people; that the forests which regulate our rivers, support our industries, and promote the fertility and productiveness of the soil should be preserved and perpetuated; that the minerals found so abundantly beneath the surface should be so used as to prolong their utility; that the beauty, healthfulness, and habitability of our country should be preserved and increased; that sources of national wealth exist for the benefit of the people, and that monopoly thereof should not be tolerated.

We commend the wise forethought of the President in sounding the note of warning as to the waste and exhaustion of the natural resources of the country, and signify our high appreciation of his action in calling this Conference to consider the same and to seek remedies therefor through coöperation of the nation and the states.

We agree that this coöperation should find expression in suitable action by the Congress within the limits of and coextensive with the national jurisdiction of the subject, and, complementary thereto, by the legislatures of the several states within the limits of and coextensive with their jurisdiction.

We declare the conviction that in the use of the national resources our independent states are interdependent and bound together by ties of mutual benefits, responsibilities, and duties.

We agree in the wisdom of future conferences between the President, members of Congress, and the governors of states on the conservation of our natural resources with a view of continued coöperation and action on the lines suggested; and to this end we advise that from time to time, as in his judgment may seem wise, the President call the governors of states and members of Congress and others into conference.

We agree that further action is advisable to ascertain the present condition of our natural resources and to promote the conservation of the same; and to that end we recommend the appointment by each state of a commission on the conservation of natural resources, to coöperate with each other and with any similar commission of the Federal Government.

We urge the continuation and extension of forest policies adapted to secure the husbanding and renewal of our diminishing timber supply, the prevention of soil erosion, the protection of headwaters, and the maintenance of the purity and navigability of our streams. We recognize that the private ownership of forest lands entails responsibilities in the interests of all the people, and we favor the enactment of laws looking to the protection and replacement of privately owned forests.

We recognize in our waters a most valuable asset of the people of the United States, and we recommend the enactment of laws looking to the conservation of water resources for irrigation, water supply, power, and navigation, to the end that navigable and source streams may be brought under complete control and fully utilized for every purpose. We especially urge on the Federal Congress the immediate adoption of a wise, active, and thorough waterway policy, providing for the prompt improvement of our streams and the conservation of their watersheds required for the uses of commerce and the protection of the interests of our people.

We recommend the enactment of laws looking to the prevention of waste in the mining and extraction of coal, oil, gas, and other minerals with a view to their wise conservation for the use of the people, and to the protection of human life in the mines.

Let us conserve the foundations of our prosperity.

THOUGHTS ON CONSERVATION

BY WILLIAM H. TAFT

WITHOUT the resources which make labor productive, American enterprise, energy, and skill would not in the past have been able to make headway against hard conditions. Our children and their children will not be able to make headway if we leave to them an impoverished country. Our land, our waters, our forests, and our minerals are the sources from which come directly or indirectly the livelihood of all of us.   The conservation of our natural resources is a question of fundamental importance to the United States now.

BY WILLIAM JENNINGS BRYAN

. . . It should be our purpose, not only to preserve the nation's resources for future generations by reducing waste to a minimum . . . we should see to it that a few of the people do not monopolize that which in equity is the property of all the people. The earth belongs to each generation, and it is as criminal to fetter future generations with perpetual franchises, making the multitude servants to a favored faction of the population, as it would be to impair, unnecessarily, the common store.

.   .   .   .

Money spent in care for the life and health of the people, in protecting the soil from erosion and from exhaustion, in preventing waste in the use of minerals of limited supply, in the reclamation of deserts and swamps, and in the preservation of forests still remaining and the planting of denuded tracts — money invested in these and in the development of waterways and in the deepening of harbors is an investment yielding an annual return.   If any of these expenditures fail to bring a return at once the money expended is like a bequest to those who come after us.   And as the parent lives for his child as well as for himself, so the good citizen provides for the future as well as for the present. This gathering will be remembered by future generations, because they as well as ourselves will be the recipients of the benefits which will flow from this conference. We have all been strengthened by communion together; our vision has been enlarged and the enthusiasm here aroused will permeate every state and every community.

BY JAMES J. HILL

"Of all the sinful wasters of man's inheritance on earth," said the late Professor Shaler, "and all are in this regard sinners, the very worst are the people of America." This is not a popular phrase, but a scientific judgment. It is borne out by facts. In the movement of modern times, which has made the world commercially a small place and has produced a solidarity of the race such as never before existed, we have come to the point where we must to a certain extent regard the natural resources of this planet as a common asset, compare them with demands now made and likely to be made upon them, and study their judicious use.

.   .   .   .

Not only the economic but the political future is involved. No people ever felt the want of work or the pinch of poverty for a long time without reaching out violent hands against their political institutions, believing that they might find in a change some

relief from their distress. . . . Every nation
finds its hour of peril when there is no longer free
access to the land, or when the land will no longer
support the people.

BY JAMES S. WHIPPLE,

*State Forest, Fish and Game Commissioner of
New York.*

The most imperative thing that we have to do
in America to-day is to save the forests of the
country.

A FEW STATISTICS

BY TREADWELL CLEVELAND, JR.

From *A Primer of Conservation,* 1908

WE ARE now cutting timber from the forests of the
United States at the rate of 500 feet B. M. a year for
every man, woman, and child. In Europe they
use only 60 board feet. At this rate, in less than
thirty years all our remaining virgin timber will be
cut. Meantime, the forests which have been cut
over are generally in a bad way for want of care;
they will produce only inferior second growth. We
are clearly over the verge of a timber famine.

This is not due to necessity, for the forests are one
of the renewable resources. Rightly used, they go
on producing crop after crop indefinitely. The
countries of Europe know this, and Japan knows it;

and their forests are becoming with time not less, but more, productive. We probably still possess sufficient forest land to grow wood enough at home to supply our own needs. If we are not blind, or wilfully wasteful, we may yet preserve our forest independence and, with it, the fourth of our great industries.

Present wastes in lumber production are enormous. Take the case of yellow pine, which now heads the list in the volume of annual cut. In 1907 it is estimated that only one-half of all the yellow pine cut during the season was used, and that the other half, amounting to 8,000,000 cords, was wasted. Such waste is typical. Mr. R. A. Long, in his address on "Forest Conservation" at the Conference on the Conservation of Natural Resources, pointed out that 20 per cent. of the yellow pine was simply left in the woods — a waste which represents the timber growing on 300,000 acres.

The rest of the waste takes place at the mill. Of course, it would never do to speak of the material rejected at the mill as waste unless this material could be turned to use by some better and more thorough form of utilization. But in many cases we know, and in many other cases we have excellent reason to believe, that most, if not all, of this material could be used with profit. It is simply a question of intelligent investigation and, more than all, of having the will to economize.

But there are other ways to conserve the forests besides cutting in half the present waste of forest products. The forests can be made to produce three or four times as rapidly as they do at present. This is true of both the virgin forests and the cut-over lands. Virgin forests are often fully stocked with first-class timber, but this stock has been laid in very slowly, on account of the wasteful competition which is carried on constantly between the rival trees. Then, too, in the virgin forest there are very many trees which have reached maturity and stopped growing, and these occupy space which, if held by younger trees, would be laying in a new stock constantly. As regards the cut-over land, severe cutting, followed by fire, has checked growth so seriously that in most cases reproduction is both poor and slow, while in many other cases there is no true forest reproduction at all at present, and there is but little hope for the future.

In addressing the Conference of Governors, the Hon. William Jennings Bryan said:

"No subject has been brought out more prominently at this Conference than the subject of forestry, and it justifies the time devoted to it, for our timberlands touch our national interests at several points. Our use of lumber is enormous, but immense as would be the inconvenience and loss caused by the absence of lumber, the consequence of the destruction of our forests would be still more disastrous to the nation. As has been shown, the timber on our mountain ranges protects our water supply. Not to speak of changes in climate which might follow the denuding of our mountains, the loss to the irrigated country could not be remedied and the damage to the streams could not be calculated."

———

RELATIONS OF TREES TO WATER

BY WILSON FLAGG

From *A Year Among the Trees*

THERE is a spot which I used to visit some years ago, that seemed to me one of the most enchanting of natural scenes. It was a level plain of about ten acres, surrounded by a narrow stream that was fed by a steep ridge forming a sort of amphitheatre round more than half its circumference. The ridge was a declivity of near a hundred feet in height, and so steep that you could climb it only by taking hold of the trees and bushes that covered it. The whole surface consisted of a thin stratum of soil deposited upon a slaty rock; but the growth of trees upon this slope was beautiful and immense, and the water that was constantly trickling from a thousand fountains kept the ground all the year green with mosses and ferns, and gay with many varieties of flowers. The soil was so rich in the meadow enclosed by this ridge, and annually fertilized by the débris washed from the hills, that the proprietor every summer filled his barns with hay, which was obtained from it without any cultivation.

I revisited this spot a few years since, after a long period of absence. A new owner, "a man of progress and enterprise," had felled the trees that grew so beautifully on the steep sides of this elevation, and valley and hill have become a dreary and unprofitable waste. The thin soil that sustained the forest, no longer protected by the trees and their undergrowth, has been washed down into the valley, leaving nothing but a bald, rocky surface, whose hideousness is scarcely relieved by a few straggling vines. The valley is also ruined; for the inundations to which it is subject after any copious rain destroy every crop that is planted upon it, and render it impracticable for tillage. It is covered with sand heaps; the little stream that glided round it, fringed with azaleas and wild roses, has disappeared, and the land is reduced to a barren pasture.

The general practice of the pioneers of civilization on this continent was to cut down the wood chiefly from the uplands and the lower slopes of the hills and mountains. They cleared those tracts which were most valuable for immediate use and cultivation. Necessity led them to pursue the very course required by the laws of nature for improving the soil and climate. The first clearings were made chiefly for purposes of agriculture; and as every farm was surrounded by a rampart of woods, it was sheltered from the force of the winds and pleasantly open to the sun. But when men began to fell the woods to supply the demands of towns and cities for fuel and lumber, these clearings were gradually deprived of their shelter, by levelling the surrounding forest and opening the country to the winds from every quarter. But the clearing of the wood from the plains, while it has rendered the climate more unstable, has not been the cause of inundations or the diminution of streams. This evil has been produced by clearing the mountains and lesser elevations having steep or rocky sides; and if this destructive work is not checked by legislation or by the wisdom of the people, plains and valleys now green and fertile will become profitless for tillage or pasture, and the advantages we shall have sacrificed will be irretrievable in the lifetime of a single generation. The same indiscriminate felling of woods has rendered many a once fertile region in Europe barren and uninhabitable, equally among the cold mountains of Norway and the sunny plains of Brittany.

Our climate suffers more than formerly from summer droughts. Many ancient streams have entirely disappeared, and a still greater number are dry in summer. Boussingault mentions a fact that clearly illustrates the condition to which we may be exposed in thousands of locations on this continent. In the Island of Ascension there was a beautiful spring, situated at the foot of a mountain which was covered with wood. By degrees the spring became less copious, and at length failed. While its waters were annually diminishing in bulk, the mountain had been gradually cleared of its forest. The disappearance of the spring was attributed to the clearing. The mountain was again planted, and as the new growth of wood increased, the spring reappeared, and finally attained its original fulness. More to be dreaded than drought, and produced by the same cause — the clearing of steep declivities of their wood — are the excessive inundations to which all parts of the country are subject.

It it were in the power of man to dispose his woods and tillage in the most advantageous manner, he might not only produce an important amelioration of the general climate, but he might diminish the frequency and severity both of droughts and inundations, and preserve the general fulness of streams. If every man were to pursue that course which would protect his own grounds from these evils, it would be sufficient to bring about this beneficent result. If each owner of land would keep all his hills and declivities, and all slopes that contain only a thin deposit of soil or a quarry, covered with forest, he would lessen his local inundations from vernal thaws and summer rains. Such a covering of wood tends to equalize the moisture that is distributed over the land, causing it, when showered upon the hills, to be retained by the mechanical action of the trees and their undergrowth of shrubs and herbaceous plants, and by the spongy surface of the soil underneath them, made porous by mosses, decayed leaves, and other débris, so that the plains and valleys have a moderate oozing supply of moisture for a long time after every shower. Without this covering, the water when precipitated upon the slopes, would immediately rush down over an unprotected surface in torrents upon the space below.

Every one has witnessed the effects of clearing the woods and other vegetation from moderate declivities in his own neighborhood. He has observed how rapidly a valley is inundated by heavy showers, if the rising grounds that form its basin are bare of trees and planted with the farmer's crops. Even grass alone serves to check the rapidity with which the water finds its way to the bottom of the slope. Let it be covered with bushes and vines, and the water flows with a speed still more diminished. Let this shrubbery grow into a forest, and the valley would never be inundated except by a long-continued and flooding rain. Woods and their undergrowth are indeed the only barriers against frequent and sudden inundations, and the only means in the economy of nature for preserving an equal fulness of streams during all seasons of the year.

At first thought, it may seem strange that the clearing of forests should be equally the cause both of drought and inundations; but these apparently incompatible facts are easily explained by considering the different effects produced by woods standing in different situations.   An excess of moisture in the valleys comes from the drainage of the hills, and the same conditions that will cause them to be dried up certain times will cause them to be flooded at others.   Nature's design seems to be to preserve a constant moderate fulness of streams and standing water.   This purpose she accomplishes by clothing the general surface of the country with wood.

THE FOREST SPONGE

From *U. S. Forest Service Circular*

WHAT child has not seen a muddy freshet?   Yet this sight, so common in the spring, is full of suggestion for a forest lesson.   The stream is discolored by the earth which it has gathered from the soil. This carries us back to the stream's source, in the forest springs.   Again, it shows us with what force the water has rushed over the exposed ground where there was no forest to shield and bind it.   In just this way the Mississippi tears down and flings into its bed, each summer, more soil than will be dredged with years of costly labor to make the Panama Canal.   An experiment with fine and coarse soils stirred quickly in a tumbler of water and then allowed to settle explains how the stream continues muddy while it runs swiftly, and how it clears again as it slackens on more level stretches, dropping the soil to the bottom. On any steep, plowed hillside, or on any railroad or trolley embankment, exposed soil may be seen washing with the rain. A forest on a mountain slope may be pictured by a cloth upon a tilted table; then if water be poured on the higher edge it will creep downward through the cloth and drip slowly from the lower edge, as would rain falling upon the forest. If now the cloth be plucked off, and the water still poured, we may observe at once what happens when such a forest is destroyed.

WARNINGS FROM HISTORY

(Compiled in 1885 *by the National Bureau of Education)*

PALESTINE

BY EMIL ROTHE

AT THE time when Joshua conquered the Promised Land, milk and honey were flowing into Canaan; that is, it was a country of wonderful fertility, blessed with a delightful climate. Both ranges of the Lebanon and its Spur Mountains were then densely covered with forests, in which the famous cedar predominated, that stately tree so masterfully and poetically described by the psalmist and the prophets. The large and continually increasing population of Palestine enjoyed comfort and abundance during centuries. But the gradual devastation of the forests, which was finally completed by the Venetians and the Genoese, brought about a general deterioration of the country. The hills of Galilee, once the rich pasturing grounds for large herds of cattle, are now sterile knobs. The Jordan became an insignificant stream, and the several beautiful smaller rivers, mentioned in the Bible, now appear as stony runs, leading off the snow and rainwater, but being completely dry during the greater part of the year. Some few valleys, in which the fertile soil washed down from the hills was deposited, have retained their old fertility, but the few cedar trees remaining as a landmark around the Maronite convent on the rocky and barren Lebanon, look lonely and mournfully upon an arid and desolate country, not fit to sustain one-sixth of such a population as it contained at the time of Solomon.

FRANCE

BY R. W. PHIPPS

IN FRANCE the aristocrats had preserved the forests. But when Jacques Bonhomme had overthrown their tyranny he proceeded to destroy the groves and forests, and in a short time he succeeded in almost staying crop growth in the fields adjacent. Wiser councils now prevail; experience has borne its fruits, and the French forests, particularly near the sea, bear witness how rapidly Providence assists a liberal, how sternly she repays a greedy and grasping, cultivator.

SPAIN

BY EMIL ROTHE

UNDER the reign of the Moorish caliphs the Iberian peninsula resembled a vast garden, yielding grain and fruit, of every known variety, in the most perfect quality, and in endless abundance, and thickly populated by a highly cultivated people. But then the sierras and mountain slopes were covered with a luxuriant growth of timber, which was afterwards wantonly destroyed under the rule of the kings. Large herds of half-wild goats and sheep prevented the spontaneous growth of trees on the neglected lands. Now nearly all the plateau-lands of Spain, being fully one-third of the entire area, are desert-like and unfit for agriculture, because of the scarcity of rain and the want of water. Another one-third of the territory is covered with worthless shrubs and thorn-bushes, and affords a scanty pasture for the merino sheep, the number of which is decreasing from year to year. The once delicious climate has become changeable and rough, since there are no more forests to break the power of the scorching Salano and the cold Galego wind. The average depth of the fine rivers that cross Spain in all directions has greatly diminished. The government, well aware of the causes of the deterioration of the soil and climate, has lately made earnest efforts, partly to replant the old forest grounds, but has met with little success, it being very difficult to make trees grow on former timber land, which has been lying waste for a longer time. It will take a full century's time and necessitate an immense outlay of money to restock Spain with sufficient timber.

SICILY

BY EMIL ROTHE

LET us look at Sicily, once the great grain reservoir for Rome. Since the island of plenty was despoiled of its forests, it gradually lost its fertility and the mildness of its climate. The ruins of proud and opulent Syracuse lay in a desert, covered by sand, which the hot sirocco carried over the Mediterranean Sea from Africa. A few isolated, well-watered, and carefully cultivated districts of very limited extension, is all that is left to remind the tourist of the bygone glory of Sicily.

THE PYRENEES MOUNTAINS

BY R. W. PHIPPS

THE desolation of mountain regions by the clearing of forests is strikingly illustrated in the Pyrenees.

Formerly the plains were cultivated, and inundations were much less frequent and less destructive than nowadays. As roads came to be opened the profit from sheep and cattle became greater, and the clearing of forests was begun to make room for pasturage and, to some extent, for timber, until by degrees the slopes of the mountains were denuded, and the rains, having nothing to hinder, began to form eroding torrents, the south slopes suffering most, because first cleared and directly exposed to the sun's heat. The extremes of flood and drouth became excessive, and extensive tracts have been ruined for present occupation from this source.

ST. HELENA

BY R. W. PHIPPS

THE Island of St. Helena, the well-known scene of Napoleon's banishment, furnishes a remarkable illustration of the connection that exists between forests and rainfall. When first discovered, in 1502, it had heavy forests. The introduction of goats, and other causes, destroyed these woodlands, until the island was almost denuded. The consequences were that in the records of the last century we find accounts of repeated and almost periodical visitations of very severe drought, occasioning various losses to cattle and crops. Towards the end of the last century, however, the governor saw the need of strenuous efforts. Gardeners were sent for, and trees from all parts of the world were planted, without regard to their character. The "Pinas Pinaster" was sown very extensively, and several plantations of this still exist. The consequences of this were discovered a few years ago as follows: "For many years past, since the general growth of our trees, we have been preserved from the scourge, and droughts such as were formerly recorded are now altogether unknown. Our fall of rain is now equal to that of England, and is spread almost evenly over the year."

OHIO

BY EMIL ROTHE

HAVE you never tried to find out why Southern Ohio has ceased to be the great fruit country *it was formerly known to be?* Why is it that we cannot raise any more peaches in our State, while they used to bring sure crops not more than a quarter of a century ago? . . . What is it that makes our climate, once so favorable for mankind and vegetation, more unsteady, from year to year? Look at the woodless hills of Southern Ohio, and you have the answer.

Let the hills be deprived of the rest of the protection which the forests afford, and half of the area of this state will be sterile in less than fifty years. The rain will wash the soil from the hilltops first, and then from the slopes; the limestone, which is now covered with productive humus, loam and clay, will be laid bare; the naked rocks will reflect the rays of the sun and increase the summer heat; the north storms will blow unhindered over the country, and every change of the wind will cause an abrupt change in the temperature. The rainfall will be diminished and become irregular. Snow and rain-water will at once run down in the valleys and cause periodical freshets, which will ultimately carry away the best part of the soil, even from the valleys. Such will be the unavoidable results of further devastation of timber.

KENTUCKY

HON. CASSIUS M. CLAY, of Kentucky, said before the American Forestry Congress at Cincinnati: "I remember, when the forests were hardly broken here, that springs of water were very frequent and perennial. The rivulets and creeks and rivers had a perpetual flow. These have now changed. The rivulets and creeks are now dried up in summer, and the fish so often caught by me in earlier years are gone. Not one spring in a thousand remains. Indian corn was generally planted in March, and the rains and exhalations of moisture from the surroundings made crops successful every year. Now, the destruction of the forests has lost to us that bed of leaves which was a perpetual reservoir of water for springs and evaporation; aided by the treading of the hard surface, the rain fall, if the same as of old, rushes off at once, sweeping the soil into the Mississippi delta. The dry winds absorb not only the ancient humidity of the air, but drink up the subsoil evaporation, so that our winters are longer, more changeable, and unendurable. Corn can hardly be safely planted till late in April, and drought too often ruins all in spite of our best efforts."

MASSACHUSETTS

PROFESSOR SARGENT, of Harvard University, who has given this question as much study as any one in America, says: "As moderators of the extremes of heat and cold, the benefits derived from extensive forests are undoubted, and that our climate is gradually changing through their destruction is apparent to the most casual observer. Our springs are later, our summers are drier, and every year becoming more so; our autumns are carried forward into winter, while our winter climate is subject to far greater changes of temperature than formerly. The total average of snowfall is perhaps as great as ever, but it is certainly less regular and covers the ground for a shorter period than formerly. Twenty years ago peaches were a profitable crop in Massachusetts; now we must depend on New Jersey and Delaware for our supply; and our apples and other orchard fruits now come from beyond the limits of New England. The failure of these and other crops in the older states is generally ascribed to the exhaustion of the soil; but with greater reason it can be referred to the destruction of the forests which sheltered us from the cold winds of the north and west, and which, keeping the soil under their shade cool in summer and warm in winter, acted at once as material barriers, and reservoirs of moisture."

THE NORTHWEST

"I HAD an opportunity," says Mr. Rothe, "to observe and study the results caused by the destruction of the forests in the Northwest. Thirty years ago steamboats drawing six feet of water made regular trips on the Upper Mississippi up to St. Paul. Now the navigation with boats of half that draft is uncertain. Nearly all the tributaries of the Upper Mississippi have also lost one-half, or even more, of their former supply of water. Inundations in the spring are now frequent, while now in the summer time the depth of many of these rivers average hardly more inches than could be measured by feet thirty years ago. Water-powers, which were formerly deemed to be inexhaustible, have entirely been abandoned, or their failing motive power has been replaced by steam. In the remembrance of the older settlers the climate of Wisconsin and Minnesota was remarkably steady, the winters were long and cold, the supply of snow ample and regular, and late frosts in the spring were unusual. Now the inhabitants complain of abrupt changes of the temperature in all seasons of the year, and of the irregularity of the snowfall. The Legislature of Wisconsin has already paid attention to these alarming facts, and has taken the preservation of existing forests, and the establishment of artificial ones into earnest consideration. By a resolution recently passed, it asks of the National Government the transfer for that purpose of all unsold public lands to the state which are now despoiled of their timber by thievish lumbermen."

ARIZONA

BY EMIL ROTHE

IN THE territory of Arizona an immense number of deserted Indian dwellings carved out of the rocks were recently discovered. The former inhabitants of the same must necessarily have been a sedative people, devoted to agriculture, but the whole district is now nearly a desert, there being no supply of water, and hills as well as plateaus and valleys are dry, stony, and nearly destitute of vegetation. This cannot have been the condition of that district when it was densely populated by hundreds and thousands of Indians. Now the only plausible solution of the ethnographical enigma which is here propounded to us, is the following: The hills and slopes there were once stocked with lumber, which was wasted by the inhabitants. The same deterioration of the country gradually took place which we notice in Palestine, Greece, and Sicily, where the people had to emigrate to avoid starvation.

But enough of the warning examples of history.

It is not too late to repair all the damage that has been done in America by the devastation of our natural forests. A regulation of the use of the timber may be effected without any injury to the legitimate lumber trade, and the replanting as well as the establishment of artificial forests, may undoubtedly be made profitable for private as well as for public enterprise. If it is remunerative to acclimatize and extensively raise American trees in Germany and France, where the soil is much higher in price than here, why should it not be lucrative to cultivate them in those parts of the United States in which the timber is scarce and precious? They grow quicker here and to greater perfection than anywhere else. Nature has lavishly provided this country with an uncommonly large number of the most valuable species of trees. There are not more than thirty-five species and distinct varieties of native trees in France which attain a height of over thirty feet, not more than sixty-five in Germany, but over one hundred and fifty in the upper part of the Mississippi

Valley alone. All Europe possesses not a single native walnut tree. (The so-called English walnut is of Asiatic origin.) We have nine varieties of hickory and two of walnut proper. You may search all the world over in vain to find a sort of timber which, in general usefulness, can rival our hickory tree. Our walnut and oak varieties alone outnumber all the varieties of trees native to France and Spain.

A benign nature has lavishly provided for this country; but does that give us a right to waste these blessings, destined for the human race of all future ages, within the short life of a few generations, like spendthrifts? Shall we adopt the most detestable motto of a modern Sardanapalus, "*Après nous le deluge*" — anticipate every thing, and leave nothing for those who will come after us? Will America's pride bear the humiliating prospect of having the immense work of culture, which so far has been achieved in this country by the most intelligent, independent, progressive, and energetic of all nations, frustrated by the unavoidable consequences of our greedy mismanagement of the natural resources of our country? Shall the future of this great republic be made uncertain by a gradual deterioration of soil and climate, or shall it forever remain the happy and comfortable home of the free? Is not the care for future generations one of the most solemn duties imposed upon us by laws of humanity and morality?

Are we worthy to enjoy the bequest of our forefathers if we are not just and liberal enough to
provide for our descendants?

"WOODMAN, SPARE THAT TREE"

HISTORY OF THE POEM

MR. MORRIS, in a letter to a friend, dated New
York, February 1, 1837, gave in substance the following account:

Riding out of town a few days since, in company
with a friend, an old gentleman, he invited me to
turn down a little, romantic woodland pass, not far
from Bloomingdale. "Your object?" inquired I.
"Merely to look once more at an old tree planted by
my grandfather long before I was born, under which
I used to play when a boy, and where my sisters
played with me. There I often listened to the good
advice of my parents. Father, mother, sisters —
all are gone; nothing but the old tree remains."
And a paleness overspread his fine countenance,
and tears came to his eyes. After a moment's
pause, he added: "Don't think me foolish. I don't
know how it is: I never ride out but I turn down this
lane to look at that old tree. I have a thousand
recollections about it, and I always greet it as a
familiar and well-remembered friend." These words
were scarcely uttered when the old gentleman cried

out, "There it is!" Near the tree stood a man with his coat off, sharpening an axe. "You're not going to cut that tree down, surely?" "Yes, but I am, though," said the woodman. "What for?" inquired the old gentleman, with choked emotion. "What for? I like that! Well, I will tell you, I want the tree for firewood." "What is the tree worth to you for firewood?" "Why, when down, about ten dollars." "Suppose I should give you that sum," said the old gentleman, "would you let it stand?" "Yes." "You are sure of that?" "Positive!" "Then give me a bond to that effect." We went into the little cottage in which my companion was born, but which is now occupied by the woodman. I drew up the bond. It was signed, and the money paid over. As we left, the young girl, the daughter of the woodman, assured us that while she lived the tree should not be cut. These circumstances made a strong impression on my mind, and furnished me with the materials for the song I send you.

———

WOODMAN, SPARE THAT TREE

BY GEORGE P. MORRIS

WOODMAN, spare that tree!
　Touch not a single bough!
In youth it sheltered me,
　And I'll protect it now.

'Twas my forefather's hand
  That placed it near his cot;
There, woodman, let it stand —
  Thy axe shall harm it not!

That old familiar tree,
  Whose glory and renown
Are spread o'er land and sea —
  And wouldst thou hew it down?
Woodman, forbear thy stroke!
  Cut not its earth-bound ties;
Oh, spare that aged oak,
  Now towering to the skies!

When but an idle boy,
  I sought its graceful shade;
In all their gushing joy
  Here, too, my sisters played.
My mother kissed me here;
  My father pressed my hand —
Forgive this foolish tear,
  But let that old oak stand!

My heart-strings round thee cling,
  Close as thy bark, old friend!
Here shall the wild-bird sing,
  And still thy branches bend.
Old tree! the storm still brave!
  And, woodman, leave the spot:
While I've a hand to save,
  Thy axe shall harm it not!

THE RESTORATION OF THE FORESTS
BY GEORGE P. MARSH
From *Man and Nature*

THE objects of the restoration of the forests are as multifarious as the motives which have led to their destruction, and as the evils which that destruction has occasioned. The planting of the mountains will diminish the frequency and violence of river inundations; prevent the formation of torrents; mitigate the extremes of atmospheric temperature, humidity and precipitation; restore dried-up springs, rivulets and sources of irrigation; shelter the fields from chilling and from parching winds; prevent the spread of miasmatic effluvia; and, finally, furnish an inexhaustible and self-renewing supply of material indispensable to so many purposes of domestic comfort, to the successful exercise of every act of peace, every destructive energy of war.

THE USES OF THE FOREST*
BY GIFFORD PINCHOT
From *A Primer of Forestry*

A FOREST, large or small, may render its service in many ways. It may reach its highest usefulness by standing as a safeguard against floods, winds,

---

* Government Printing Office, 1905.

snow slides, moving sands, or especially against the dearth of water in the streams. A forest used in this way is called a protection forest, and is usually found in the mountains, or on bleak, open plains, or by the sea. Forests which protect the headwaters of streams used for irrigation, and many of the larger windbreaks of the Western plains, are protection forests. The Adirondack and Catskill woodlands were regarded as protection forests by the people of the State of New York when they forbade, in the constitution of 1895, the felling, destruction, or removal of any trees from the State Forest Preserve.

A farmer living directly on the produce of his land would find his woodlot most useful to him when it supplied the largest amount of wood for his peculiar needs, or the best grazing for his cattle. A railroad holding land which it did not wish to sell would perhaps find it most useful when it produced the greatest number of ties and bridge timbers. In both cases the forest would render its best service by producing the greatest quantity of valuable material. This is the central idea upon which the national forests of France are managed.

The greatest return in money may be the service most desired of the forest. If a farmer wished to sell the product of his woodlot instead of consuming it himself, his woodland would be useful to him just in proportion to its net yield in money. This is true also in the case of any owner of a forest who wishes to dispose of its product, but who cannot, or will not, sell the forest itself. State forests, like those in the Adirondacks, often render their best service, in addition to their usefulness as protection forests, by producing the greatest net money return. Regarded as an investment of capital, a forest is most useful when it yields the highest rate of interest. A forest whose owner could sell it if he chose, but prefers to hold it as productive capital, is useful in proportion to the interest it yields on the money invested in it. Thus, an acre of sprout land may be worth only $5, while the investment in adjoining land stocked with old trees may be $50 an acre. This is the view which controls the management of state forests in Germany. Lumbermen also regard timberland as an investment, but usually they take no care except for the yield at the moment. They disregard the future yield altogether, and in consequence the forest loses its capital value, or may even be totally destroyed. Well-managed forests, on the other hand, are made to yield their service always without endangering the future yield, and usually to its great advantage. Like the plant of a successful manufacturer, a forest should increase in productiveness and value year by year.

Under various circumstances, then, a forest may yield its best return in protection, in wood, grass, or other forest products, in money, or in interest on the capital it represents. But whichever of these ways of using the forest may be chosen in any given case, the fundamental idea in forestry is that of perpetuation by wise use; that is, of making the forest yield the best service possible at the present in such a way that its usefulness in the future will not be diminished, but rather increased.

FOUR REQUIREMENTS FOR THE BEST SERVICE

BY GIFFORD PINCHOT

A FOREST well managed under the methods of practical forestry will yield a return in one of the ways just mentioned. There are, however, four things a forest must have before it can be in condition to render the best service.

The first of these is protection, especially against fire, overgrazing, and thieves, for without such protection no investment is secure and the most skilful management is of little effect.

The second is strong and abundant reproduction. A forest without young growth is like a family without children. It will speedily die out.

The third requirement is a regular supply of trees ripe for the axe. This can be secured only by the right porportion of each of the smaller sizes constantly coming on in the growing forest.

The fourth requirement is growing space enough for every tree, so that the forest as a whole may

not only produce wood as fast as possible, but the
most valuable sort of wood as well.   If the trees
stand too far apart, their trunks will be short and
thickly covered with branches, the lumber cut from
them will be full of knots, and its value will be
small.   If, on the other hand, the trees stand too
closely together, although their trunks will be tall
and clear of branches, they will be small in diameter,
and for that reason low in value.   With the right
amount of growing space, trees grow both tall
and of good diameter, and their trunks supply
lumber of higher price because it is wide and clear.

WHAT DO WE PLANT WHEN WE PLANT THE TREE?

BY HENRY ABBEY

WHAT do we plant when we plant the tree?
We plant the ship which will cross the sea,
We plant the mast to carry the sails,
We plant the planks to withstand the gales —
The keel, the keelson, and beam and knee —
We plant the ship when we plant the tree.

What do we plant when we plant the tree?
We plant the houses for you and me.
We plant the rafters, the shingles, the floors,
We plant the studding, the lath, the doors
The beams and siding, all parts that be,
We plant the house when we plant the tree.

What do we plant when we plant the tree?
A thousand things that we daily see.
We plant the spire that out-towers the crag,
We plant the staff for our country's flag,
We plant the shade from the hot sun free;
We plant all these when we plant the tree.

————

FACTS ABOUT TREES FOR THE LITTLE ONES
From *Primary Education*

(*A Recitation*)

1. Cutting down trees spoils the beauty of the landscape. I would not like to live where there were no trees.

2. There are few birds where there are no trees. They have no place to make their homes.

3. Taking away the trees takes away the protection from our tender fruit trees.

4. Where there are no trees the snows melt and go off too rapidly; the moisture that should sink into the soil is carried away in floods.

5. Because our forests are taken away we have severe droughts every year.

6. One full-grown elm tree gives out fifteen tons of moisture in twenty-four hours. A large sunflower plant gives off three pints of water in one day.

7. The trees give us lumber, fuel, wood, pulp for newspapers, cork, bark for tanning, wild fruits,

nuts, resin, turpentine, oils, and various products for medicines.

8. We should have greater extremes of heat and cold if it were not for the trees and forests.

9. The leaves of trees catch the rain and hold it a little while; then they drop the water a little at a time; this is better for the ground.

10. The old leaves make a deep sponge carpet in the woods, and this keeps the ground from freezing. If the earth does not freeze it takes up the rain better.

11. We might have dangerous floods if we did not have trees. The trunks and roots of trees stop the water that comes pouring down the hillside.

12. I will be very careful not to hurt any tree, but will call every tree my friend.

FOREST PRESERVATION AND RESTORATION

BY JAMES S. WHIPPLE

MY DESIRE in writing this article is to interest my readers in the protection of our forests, fish, game animals, and game and song birds. It is, of course, most important that the forest should be preserved, for upon its life depends largely the life of the fish, and the game animals and birds.

The necessity for preserving the forest for commercial purposes alone is apparent. There are on public and private lands in this state of New York abou t41,000,000,000 feet of timber, board measure. Last year there were cut and manufactured in the state 1,500,000,000 feet of lumber, taken, of course, from private lands, since a clause in the Constitution prohibits the removal of timber from state lands. But at the same rate of cutting, all the timber in the state, public and private, would not last more than thirty years. To be sure, there is considerable growth going on in the forest, but this is more than offset by the increasing demand for lumber on account of the rapidly growing population, and the increasing use of wood in manufacturing.

The first settlers along the Hudson knew something about practical forestry, and the necessity of forest preservation. They had learned it in Holland. On their arrival here they found a great, deep, dark forest stretching westward, how far they did not know. They found it a hindrance and constant threat. It hid their enemies. In órder to build, to plant, and to make a place to live, it had to be cut down and removed. It was about this first cutting that the poet wrote,

> His echoing axe the settler swung
>   Amid the sea-like solitude,
> And rushing, thundering down were flung
>   The Titans of the wood.

The early settlers soon forgot their forestry principles, and the second generation knew little and cared less about them. Billions of feet of good timber were deliberately burned to ashes to get it out of the way. There was great waste, wanton waste, because much timber was taken from lands that could never be used for tillage.

An examination of the early colonial laws, the acts of Parliament to the mother country, shows that as far back as 1640 there was a very correct idea of the value of the splendid pine forest that covered the lands of the new world. Yet nothing practical was done until 1885, when a commission was appointed in this state, which commenced the work now carried on by the department which I have the honor to represent. A hundred years previously, however, a commission had been appointed to investigate and report upon the forests of the state and devise some plan to acquire and save some of the forest lands. But nothing came of it and no legislation followed. Surely in this case the Legislature cannot be accused of hasty legislation.

If our forests were converted into lumber they would be worth many millions of dollars, but they are worth many millions more if left standing, and managed according to forestry principles. Not only will they then continue to grow, but they will protect the headwaters of our streams, regulate temperature, protect from hot and cold winds, serve as a health and pleasure resort, and furnish a home for game, fish, and song birds.

It is time to call a halt on forest destruction, and order a forward march on forest restoration. The great pines once used for spars and planks in the king's ships are all gone. The great oak forests are seen no more. Their grandeur and beauty are known only in legend, song, and story. But a worse disaster is close at hand. In a few years we shall experience the inconvenience of a wood famine. If we would minimize its effects, and prevent the dire results of forest destruction upon the streams, fish and game, we must bestir ourselves.

At least two lines of action it is certainly our duty to follow. The state should immediately acquire a million acres more land in the Adirondacks, and five hundred thousand more acres in the Catskills. Then, not only should the state plant millions of trees each year upon its denuded lands, but it should encourage private owners to reforest all ground not good for agriculture. The State should raise and distribute seedling trees, at actual cost, or, if possible, free of cost, to all persons who will plant them according to directions furnished by the state.

SPARE THE TREES

BY MADAME MICHELET

ALAS, in how many places is the forest which once lent us shade, nothing more than a memory. The grave and noble circle which adorned the mountain is every day contracting. Where you come in hope of seeing life, you find but the image of death. Oh, who will really undertake the defense of the trees, and rescue them from senseless destruction? Who will eloquently set forth their manifold mission, and their active and incessant assistance in the regulation of the laws which rule our globe? Without them, it seems delivered over to blind destiny, which will involve it again into chaos. The motive powers and purifiers of the atmosphere through the respiration of their foliage, avaricious collectors, to the advantage of future ages, of the solar heat, it is they which pacify the storm and avert its most disastrous consequences. In the low-lying plains, which have no outlet for their waters, the trees, long before the advent of man, drained the soil by their roots, forcing the stagnant waters to descend and construct at a lower depth their useful reservoirs. And now, on the abrupt declivities, they consolidate the crumbling soil, check and break the torrent, control the melting of the snows, and preserve to the meadows the fertile humidity which in due time will overspread them with a sea of flowers. And is not this enough? To watch over the life of the plant and its general harmony, is it not to watch over the safety of humanity? The tree, again, was created for the nurture of man, to assist him in his industries and his arts. It is owing to the tree, to its soul, earth-buried for so many centuries, and now restored to light, that we have secured the wings of the steam engine. Thank heaven for the trees! With my feeble voice I claim for them the gratitude of man.

VIII

EXERCISES

AN ARBOR DAY EXERCISE

First Pupil.

To HIM who in the love of nature holds
Communion with her visible forms, she speaks
A various language; for his gayer hours
She has a voice of gladness, and a smile
And eloquence of beauty, and she glides
Into his darker musings with a mild
And healing sympathy, that steals away
Their sharpness, ere he is aware.

—BRYANT.

Second Pupil.

For Nature beats in perfect tune,
And rounds with rhyme her every rune,
Whether she work in land or sea,
Or hide underground her alchemy.
Thou can'st not wave thy staff in air
Or dip thy paddle in the lake,
But it carves the bow of beauty there,
And the ripples in rhymes the oar forsake.
The wood is wiser far than thou;
The wood and wave each other know.
Not unrelated, unaffied,

But to each thought and thing allied,
Is perfect Nature's every part,
Rooted in the mighty Heart.
                                    —EMERSON.

Third Pupil.

One impulse from a vernal wood
    May teach you more of man,
Of moral evil and of good,
    Than all the sages can.
                                    —WORDSWORTH.

Fourth Pupil.

Faint murmurs from the pine-tops reach my ear,
As if a harp-string — touched in some far sphere—
Vibrating in the lucid atmosphere,
Let the soft south wind waft its music here.
                                    —T. B. ALDRICH.

Fifth Pupil.

Old trees in their living state are the only things
that money cannot command. Rivers leave their
beds, run into cities and traverse mountains for it;
obelisks and arches, palaces and temples, amphi-
theaters and pyramids rise up like exhalations at its
bidding. Even the free spirit of man, the only thing
great on earth, crouches and cowers in its presence.
It passes away and vanishes before venerable trees.
                                    —LANDOR.

TREES

ANONYMOUS

For a Class Exercise

First Pupil.

Forest trees have always "haunted me like a passion." Let us summon a few of them, prime favorites, and familiar to the American forest.

Second Pupil.

First the *Aspen*, what soft silver-gray tints on its leaves, how smooth its mottled bark, its whole shape how delicate and sensitive!

Third Pupil.

Next the *Elm*, how noble the lift and droop of its branches; it has the shape of the Greek vase, such lavish foliage, running down the trunk to the very roots, as if a rich vine were wreathed around it!

Fourth Pupil.

Then the *Maple*, what a splendid cupola of leaves it builds up into the sky, and in autumn, its crimson is so rich, one might term it the blush of the woods!

Fifth Pupil.

And the *Beech*, how cheerful its snow-spotted trunk looks in the deep woods! The pattering of the beechnut upon the dead leaves, in the hazy days of our Indian summer, makes a music like the dripping of a rill, in the mournful forest.

Sixth Pupil.

The *Birch* is a great favorite of mine. How like a shaft of ivory it gleams in the daylight woods! How the flame of moonlight kindles it into columned pearl!

Seventh Pupil.

Now the *Oak*, what a tree it is! First a tiny needle rising grandly toward the sun, a wreath of green to endure for ages. The child gathers the violet at its foot; as a boy he pockets its acorns; as a man he looks at its heights towering up and makes it the emblem of his ambition.

Eighth Pupil.

We now come to the *Pine*, of all my greatest favorite. The oak may be king of the lowlands, but the pine is king of the hills. There he lifts his haughty front like the warrior he is, and when he is roused to meet the onslaught of the storm, the battle-cry he sends down the wind is heard above all the voices of the greenwood.

Ninth Pupil.

We will merely touch, in passing, upon the *Hemlock*, with its masses of evergreen needles, and the *Cedar* with its misty blue berries; and the *Sumac* with its clusters of crimson, and the *Witch-hazel*, smiling at winter, with its curled, sharp-cut flowers of golden velvet.

Tenth Pupil

Did you ever, while wandering in the forest about the first of June, have your eyes dazzled at a distance with what you supposed to be a tree ladened with snow? It was the *Dogwood*, glittering in its white blossoms. It brightens the last days of spring with its floral beauty.

Eleventh Pupil.

While admiring the dogwood, an odor of exquisite sweetness may salute you; and, if at all conversant in tree knowledge, you will know it is the *Basswood*, clustered with yellow blossoms, golden bells pouring out such strong, delicious fragrance, you must all realize the idea of Shelley.

All.

And the hyacinths, purple and white and blue,
Which flung from its bells a sweet peal anew,
Of music so delicate, soft and intense,
It was felt like an odor within the sense.

ARBOR DAY ALPHABET

BY ADA SIMPSON SHERWOOD

(*For twenty-six small children*)

(Let each child wear or carry his letter, made of green leaves, and, as far as possible, carry branches or twigs of the tree of which he speaks.)

A is for *apple tree*, sweet with bloom,
　　Or laden with golden fruit.

B is for *beech*, with thick, cool shade,
　　And the *birches* of ill repute.

C is for *chestnut* and *cedar* fair,
　　And *cypress*, where sorrows abide.

D is for *dogwood*, whose fair white tents
　　Are pitched by the riverside.

E is for *elm*, New England's pride;
　　True patriot's love they stir.

F is for *fig tree* of the South,
　　And the cone-shaped northern *fir*.

G is for *gum tree*, so well known
　　To the southern girls and boys.

H is for *hemlock*, steadfast tree,
　　And for *holly* with Christmas joys.

I is for *ironwood*, firm and strong,
　　And the *ivy* that twines around.

J is for *juniper*, low and green,
　　Where purple berries are found.

K is for *king* of the forest grand,
The *oak* must wear the crown.

L is for thorny *locust*, the *larch*,
And the *linden* of fair renown.

M is for *maple*, favorite one,
The queen of all the trees.

N is for *Norway pine*, which still
Is whispering to the breeze.

O is for *orange*, blooming for brides,
And the *olive*, yielding rich oil.

P is for *poplar*, reaching high,
And the *palm* of the southern soil.

Q is for *quince*, in our gardens low,
With its fruit so sour and green.

R is for *redwood*, giant trees,
The largest that can be seen.

S is for *spruce*, bright evergreen,
And the silvery *sycamore*.

T is for *tulip tree*, broad and high,
With its beautiful tulip-like flower.

U is for *upas*, tropical tree,
With its fabled poisoned air.

V is for *vines* that cling to the tree,
For friendship, strength, and care.

W is for *walnut*, dark and firm,
And for *willow*, faithful and true.

X is *xanthoxylum*, bitter bane
Whose virtue is strengthening power.
Y is for *yew tree*, dwelling alone,
Friendless and sad we know.
Z is for *zenith*, the point above,
Toward which the trees all grow.

———

SONG

(Tune, "Buy my Flowers")

Apple, beech, and cedar fair,
Fir and hemlock, worthy pair,
Elm and oak and maple queen,
Lords and ladies robed in green!
On this joyous Arbor Day
Duty's pleasant call obey.
Plant the trees,
Plant the trees this Arbor Day.

Grand old trees, we love them all!
Pine and poplar waving tall,
Tulip tree and walnut, too,
Willow sad and lonely yew.
On this joyous Arbor Day
Duty's pleasant call obey,
Plant the trees,
Plant the trees this Arbor Day.

VOICES OF THE TREES

BY PROFESSOR W. H. BENEDICT

First Pupil.

I am familiar to all as the American Elm.   I have been called the Queen of the Forest, and stand without a rival at the head of the list of ornamental deciduous-leaved trees.   I claim this rank on account of rapid growth, and the graceful and majestic beauty of my drooping branches.

Second Pupil.

I am the celebrated Birch.   I am a useful factor in the cause of education, though not now so commonly found in the schoolroom as in former years.

Third Pupil.

I am called the Chestnut.   All botanists of the present day agree that I am first cousin to the Oak. I am well known for valuable timber and a good crop of edible nuts.   I am a great friend of the boys and girls.   Sometimes naughty boys seek me rather than the schoolroom.   Of course no such boys live in Elmira.

Fourth Pupil.

I am known as the Willow.   I live near the water, and my wood is made into the strongest things —

artificial limbs, tooth-picks, ball clubs, and gun-powder. Some of us are called Pussy Willows.

CONCERT RECITATION

O willow, why forever weep,
  As one who mourns an endless wrong?
What hidden woe can lie so deep?
  What utter grief can last so long?

Mourn on forever, unconsoled,
  And keep your secret, faithful tree.
No heart in all the world can hold
  A sweeter grace than constancy.

Fifth Pupil.

I rejoice in the name of the Pine. I am the musician among the trees. I sing only when the spirit moves. You may know when that is by the peculiar swaying of my head.

Sixth Pupil.

Behold in me the Sugar Maple and a favorite ornamental tree. People love me because I am possessed of sweetness. I claim to have made more boys and girls happy than any other tree. I have many changes in dress — wearing in the spring the softest shade of every color, in the summer the purest emerald, and in the autumn the most brilliant yellow. My wood is used for furniture, floors, and for furnishing the interior of houses, and after the houses are finished few can warm them better than I.

Seventh Pupil.

Behold in me the Beech. Upon my smooth, gray bark many a heart-history has been carved. The poet Campbell tells it so beautifully:

CONCERT RECITATION

Thrice twenty summers have I stood,
Since youthful lovers in my shade
Their vows of truth and rapture paid,
And, on my trunk's surviving frame,
Carved many a long-forgotten name.

Eighth Pupil.

They call me Basswood. I am a fine shade tree, my home a moist, rich soil. My fragrant flowers furnish a great amount of excellent honey for the bees at a time when most other flowers have disappeared. My timber is soft, light, and tough, and not apt to split; good for cabinet work, boxes, and broom handles.

Ninth Pupil.

Recognize in me the Hickory. If you want a wood that is good for buggies, axe handles, barrel hoops, a wood like iron, call upon me. You will have all the nuts you want thrown into the bargain. Once upon a time there was a President of the country who had so many of my qualities that they called him Old Hickory.

Tenth Pupil.

You see before you the Black Spruce. I abound in swamps. I am often used for Christmas trees on festive occasions, and boys and girls search me over for a supply of first-class gum. I am not responsible, though, for all the gum that goes by my name. Within a few years my wood has been largely used to make white paper.

CONCERT RECITATION

I love thee in the spring,
Earth-crownèd forest! when amid the shades
The gentle South first waves her odorous wing,
And joy fills all the glades.

In the hot summer-time,
With deep delight, the somber aisles I roam,
Or, soothed by some cool brook's melodious chime,
Rest on thy verdant loam.

But oh, when autumn's hand
Hath marked thy beauteous foliage for the grave,
How doth thy splendor, as entranced I stand,
My willing heart enslave!

SCRIPTURE SELECTIONS

May be arranged for a responsive service

GENESIS

i. 11.   And God said, Let the earth bring forth the fruit tree, yielding fruit after his kind.

12.   And the earth brought forth the tree, yielding fruit whose seed was in itself after his kind.   And God said that it was good.

29.   And God said, Behold I have given you every tree in which is the fruit of a tree yielding seed; to you it shall be for meat.

ii. 8.   And the Lord God planted a garden eastward in Eden, and there He put the man whom he had formed.

9.   And out of the ground made the Lord God to grow every tree that is pleasant to the sight, and good for food; the tree of life also in the midst of the garden, and the tree of knowledge of good and evil.

DEUTERONOMY

viii. 7, 8, 9.   For the Lord thy God bringeth thee into a good land; a land of brooks of water, of fountains and depths that spring out of valleys and hills; a land of wheat and barley, and vines, and fig trees, and pomegranates; a land of oil, olive, and honey; a land wherein thou shalt eat bread without scarceness, thou shalt not lack anything in it; a land whose stones are iron, and out of whose hills thou mayest dig brass.

I. CHRONICLES

xvi. 33. Then shall the trees of the wood sing out at the presence of the Lord.

JOB

xiv. 7, 8, 9. For there is hope of a tree, if it be cut down, that it will sprout again, and that the tender branch thereof will not cease, though the root thereof wax old in the earth; and the stock thereof die in the ground; yet through the scent of water it will bud and bring forth boughs like a plant.

PSALMS

i. 1, 2, 3. Blessed is the man whose delight is in the law of the Lord. He shall be like a tree planted by the streams of water that bringeth its fruit in its season, whose leaf also doth not wither, and whatsoever he doeth shall prosper.

xcii. 12. The righteous shall flourish like the palm tree; he shall grow like a cedar in Lebanon.

civ. 16, 17. The trees of the Lord are full of sap; the cedars of Lebanon which he hath planted;

where the birds make their nests; as for the stork, the fir trees are her house.

cxlviii. 9. Mountains and all hills; fruitful trees, and all cedars.

13. Let them praise the name of the Lord.

PROVERBS

iii. 18. Wisdom is a tree of life to them that lay hold upon her; and happy is every one that retaineth her.

xi. 30. The fruit of the righteous is a tree of life.

xiii. 12. Hope deferred maketh the heart sick; but when the desire cometh, it is a tree of life.

xv. 4. A wholesome tongue is a tree of life.

THE SONG OF SOLOMON

ii. 3. As the apple tree among the trees of the wood, so is my beloved among the sons. I sat down under his shadow with great delight, and his fruit was sweet to my taste.

ISAIAH

lv. 12. All the trees of the field shall clap their hands.

13. Instead of the thorn shall come up the fir tree, and instead of the brier shall come up the myrtle tree, and it shall be to the Lord for a name.

lx. 13.   The glory of Lebanon shall come unto thee, the fir tree, the pine tree and the box together.

lxi. 3.   That they might be called trees of righteousness, the planting of the Lord, that he might be glorified.

St. Matthew

vii. 17.   Even so every good tree bringeth forth good fruit; but a corrupt tree bringeth forth evil fruit.

vii. 18.   A good tree cannot bring forth evil fruit, neither can a corrupt tree bring forth good fruit.

19.   Every tree that bringeth not forth good fruit is hewn down, and cast into the fire.

20.   Wherefore by their fruits ye shall know them.

Revelation

ii. 7.   . . . To him that overcometh will I give to eat of the tree of life, which is in the midst of the paradise of God.

xxi. 10.   And he carried me away in the spirit to a great and high mountain, and showed me that great city, the holy Jerusalem. . . .

xxii. 2.   In the midst of the street of it, and on either side of the river, was there the tree of life, which bare twelve manner of fruits, and yielded her fruit every month; and the leaves of the tree were for the healing of the nations.

SONGS AND CHORUS OF THE FLOWERS

BY LEIGH HUNT

ROSES

We are blushing Roses,
  Bending with our fulness,
'Midst our close-capped sister buds
  Warming the green coolness.

Whatsoe'er of beauty
  Yearns and yet reposes —
Blush, and bosom, and sweet breath
  Took a shape in Roses.

Hold one of us lightly,
  See from what a slender
Stalk we bow'd in heavy blooms,
  And roundness rich and tender.

Know you not our only
  Rival flower — the human?
Loveliest weight on lightest foot,
  Joy-abundant woman?

LILIES

We are Lilies fair,
  The flower of virgin light;
Nature held us forth and said,
  "Lo! my thoughts of white."

Ever since then, angels
Hold us in their hands;
You may see them where they take
In pictures their sweet stands.

Like the garden's angels
Also do we seem,
And not the less for being crown'd
With a golden dream.

Could you see around us
The enamoured air,
You would see it pale with bliss
To hold a thing so fair.

SWEETBRIER

Wild-rose, Sweetbrier, Eglantine —
All these pretty names are mine,
And scent in every leaf is mine,
And a leaf for all is mine,
And the scent — oh, that's divine!
Happy sweet and pungent-fine,
Pure as dew and picked as wine.

As the Rose in gardens dress'd,
Is the lady self-possess'd;
I'm the lass in simple vest,
The country lass whose blood's the best;
Were the beams that thread the brier

In the morn with golden fire
Scented too, they'd smell like me —
All Elysian pungency.

VIOLETS

We are Violets blue,
    For our sweetness found
Careless in the mossy shades,
    Looking on the ground.
Love's dropp'd eyelids and a kiss —
Such our breath and blueness is.

Io, the mild shape
    Hidden by Jove's fears,
Found us first i' the sward, when she
    For hunger stoop'd in tears.
"Wheresoe'er her lip she sets,"
Jove said, "be breaths call'd Violets."

POPPIES

We are slumberous Poppies,
    Lords of Lethe downs,
Some awake, and some asleep,
    Sleeping in our crowns.
What perchance our dreams may know,
Let our serious beauty show.

Central depth of purple,
    Leaves more bright than rose,
Who shall tell what brightest thought

Out of darkest grows?
Who, through what funereal pain
Souls to love and peace attain?

Visions aye are on us,
    Unto eyes of power,
Pluto's always-setting sun,
    And Proserpina's bower.
There, like bees, the pale souls come
For our drink with drowsy hum.

Taste, ye mortals, also;
    Milky-hearted we;
Taste, but with a reverend care;
    Active, patient be.
Too much gladness brings to gloom
Those who on the gods presume.

CHORUS OF FLOWERS

We are the sweet flowers,
Born of sunny showers;
(Think, whene'er you see us, what our beauty saith);
Utterance, mute and bright,
Of some unknown delight,
We fill the air with pleasure by our simple breath:
All who see us love us —
We befit all places;
Unto sorrow we give smiles — and, unto graces,
    races.

Think of all our treasures,
Matchless works and pleasures,
Every one a marvel, more than thought can say;
Then think in what bright showers
We thicken fields and bowers,
And with what heaps of sweetness half stifle wanton
    May;
Think of the mossy forests
By the bee-birds haunted,
And all those Amazonian plains, lone lying as
    enchanted.

Trees *themselves* are ours;
Fruits are born of flowers;
Beech, and roughest nut were blossoms in the spring;
The lusty bee knows well
The news, and comes pell-mell,
And dances in the gloomy thicks with darksome
    antheming:
Beneath the very burden
Of planet-pressing ocean
We wash our smiling cheeks in peace — a thought for
    meek devotion.

Who shall say that flowers
Dress not heaven's own bowers?
Who its love, without us, can fancy — or sweet floor?
    Who shall even dare
    To say we sprang not there —

And came not down, that Love might bring one piece
   of heaven the more?
Oh, pray believe that angels
From those blue dominions
Brought us in their white laps down, 'twixt their
   golden pinions.

NEW YORK STATE PROGRAMME, 1889
PROGRAMME

Caution: Do not make the programme too long.

(This programme is intended to be merely suggestive, and may be varied as tastes, circumstances and
opportunities may permit. The ingenuity of teachers
is relied upon to make such changes as may be
necessary to interest in some way all grades of
pupils, care being taken to make the exercises as
full of life as possible.)

Suggestions: The order of recitations noted
below may be greatly varied. Different scholars
may recite one verse each of a stated poem, all
reciting the last verse in concert. "The Planting
of the Apple Tree" may appropriately be used in
this connection, to be followed by singing in concert,
"Swinging 'neath the Old Apple Tree."

A very appropriate exercise for younger children
may be made under the head "Breezes from the
Forest," or "Voices of the Trees," in which many
children may take part, each pupil reciting a verse

especially prepared. The first may begin: "I am the sugar maple," etc., other pupils speaking as other trees. The following is given as an illustration of this plan, adopted at Port Henry, N. Y., in 1888: "I am the sugar maple, and a favorite ornamental tree. People love me because I am possessed of sweetness. I claim to have made more boys and girls happy than any other tree. I have many changes of dress — wearing in spring the softest shade of every color, in the summer the purest emerald, and in the autumn the most brilliant yellow. My wood is used for furniture, floors, and for furnishing the interior of houses, and after the houses are finished, few can warm them better than I."

The expression in the opening sentence may be varied, as "I am known as" — "They call me," etc.

Older pupils might interest themselves in organizing as a "Convention of Trees," each pupil representing a tree familiar in the locality, and to be called by its name. Officers to be chosen by name of trees, and remarks and discussions participated in by members of the Convention, to be recognized by names of trees.

Compositions may be prepared by older students upon various subjects connected with trees; as, for example, their uses for shade, for ornament, for producing fuel, lumber, etc.; their influence in increasing the rainfall, retaining moisture, modifying the temperature, etc.; their value in furnishing food, materials for clothing; ropes, medicines, oils, homes for the birds, houses, furniture, etc.; their value as defense against storms, from avalanches in Switzerland, and in preserving health by counteracting the influences of malaria, etc.

Compositions may also be written on the size of trees, trees in history, care of trees, enemies of trees, the kinds and habits of native trees, kinds of ornamental trees; also, a description of the tree chosen for planting, its characteristics, usefulness, etc.; upon varieties of shrubs that are valuable for landscape gardening, their habits of growth, flowering, etc. The same exercises may be extended to include the vines or flower seeds or flowering plants that may be selected for cultivation.

1. DEVOTIONAL EXERCISES:

(a) Reading of Scripture: (b) Prayer. (c) Song.
(Note. See Scripture lesson given elsewhere. This may be read by one person, or different scholars may each repeat a verse or a sentence. Or it may be made a responsive service, the teacher repeating one sentence, and scholars the next).

2. READING OF THE LAW ESTABLISHING ARBOR DAY.

3. READING OF DEPARTMENT CIRCULAR, AND OF LETTERS IN REFERENCE TO ARBOR DAY.
(Note. Many teachers and others in charge

of exercises may choose to invite letters appropriate to the occasion, from prominent persons in the different localities who are unable to be present.)

4. SONG.

5. RECITATIONS. By different pupils.

First Pupil.

"The groves were God's first temples
    Ere man learned
To hew the shaft, and lay the architrave
And spread the roof above them — ere he framed
The lofty vault, to gather and roll back
The round of anthems — in the darkling wood,
Amidst the cool and silence, he knelt down
And offered to the Mightiest solemn thanks
And supplications."

            —BRYANT.

Second Pupil.

"I shall speak of trees, as we see them, love them, adore them in the fields where they are alive, holding their green sunshades over our heads, talking to us with their hundred thousand whispering tongues, looking down on us with that sweet meekness which belongs to huge but limited organisms — which one sees most in the patient posture, the outstretched arms, and the heavy drooping robes of these vast beings, endowed with life, but not with soul — which outgrow us and outlive us, but stand helpless, poor things — while nature dresses and undresses them."

—HOLMES.

Third Pupil.

"Give fools their gold and knaves their power;
Let fortune's bubbles rise and fall;
Who sows a field, or trains a flower,
Or plants a tree, is more than all.
For he who blesses most is blest;
And God and man shall own his worth;
Who toils to leave as his bequest
An added beauty to the earth."

—WHITTIER.

Fourth Pupil.

"There is something nobly simple and pure in a taste for the cultivation of forest trees. It argues, I think, a sweet and generous nature to have this strong relish for the beauties of vegetation, and this friendship for the hardy and glorious sons of the forest. There is a grandeur of thought connected with this part of rural economy. . . . He who plants an oak looks forward to future ages, and plants for posterity. Nothing can be less selfish than this."

—IRVING.

Fifth Pupil.

"What conqueror in any part of 'Life's broad field of battle' could desire a more beautiful, a more noble, or a more patriotic monument than a tree planted by the hands of pure and joyous children, as a memorial of his achievements?"

—Lossing.

Sixth Pupil.

"Oh! Rosalind, these trees shall be my books,
And in their barks my thoughts I'll character,
That every eye which in this forest looks,
Shall see thy virtue witnessed everywhere."

—Shakespeare.

Seventh Pupil.

"There is something unspeakably cheerful in a spot of ground which is covered with trees, that smiles amidst all the rigors of winter, and gives us a view of the most gay season in the midst of that which is the most dead and melancholy."

—Addison.

Eighth Pupil.

"As the leaves of trees are said to absorb all noxious qualities of the air, and to breath forth a purer atmosphere, so it seems to me as if they drew from us all sordid and angry passions, and breathed forth peace and philanthropy."

—Irving.

Ninth Pupil.

"I care not how men trace their ancestry,
To ape or Adam; let them please their whim;

But I in June am midway to believe
A tree among my far progenitors,
Such sympathy is mine with all the race,
Such mutual recognition vaguely sweet
There is between us."

—LOWELL.

Tenth Pupil.

"Trees have about them something beautiful and attractive even to the fancy. Since they cannot change their plan, are witnesses of all the changes that take place around them; and as some reach a great age, they become, as it were, historical monuments, and, like ourselves, they have a life growing and passing away, not being inanimate and unvarying like the fields and rivers. One sees them passing through various stages, and at last, step by step, approaching death, which makes them look still more like ourselves."

—HUMBOLDT.

Eleventh Pupil.

"Summer or winter, day or night,
The woods are an ever new delight;
They give us peace, and they make us strong,
Such wonderful balms to them belong;
So, living or dying, I'll take my ease
Under the trees, under the trees."

STODDARD.

6. READING OR DECLAMATION.
7. SONG.
8. ADDRESS. "Our School-houses and our Homes, How to beautify them."
   (Note. Any other appropriate subject may be selected.)
9. SONG.
10. BRIEF ESSAYS. By different scholars.
    (First scholar may choose for subject, "My Favorite Tree is the Oak," and give reasons. Other scholars may follow, taking for subjects the Elm, Maple, Beech, Birch, Ash, etc. These essays should be very short.)
11. SONG.
12. VOTING ON THE QUESTION. "What is the Favorite State Tree?"
13. READING OR RECITATION.
14. SONG.
15. ORGANIZATION OF LOCAL "Shade-Tree Planting Association."
    (See suggestions under this head elsewhere.)
    (Note. The scholars should at least appoint a committee to serve for a year to see that trees planted are properly cared for.)
16. SONG.

PROGRAMME — AT THE TREE

Suggestions: Arriving at the place designated for the planting of a tree, everything should be found in readiness by previous preparation, in order that there may be no delay. By arrangement, the tree should be dedicated to some particular person as may have been decided. It would be well to have printed or painted on tin or wood, and attached to the tree, the name of the person to whom it is dedicated.

After a marching song has been sung on the way to the tree, the following order of exercises is suggested:

1. PLACE THE TREE CAREFULLY IN POSITION. (See 5, below).
   (Note. When advisable, the tree may be placed in position in advance of the exercises.)
2. SONG.
3. A brief statement by the teacher or another concerning the person to whom the tree is dedicated.
4. When practicable — recital of quotations from the writings of the person thus honored.
5. Let each pupil in the class, or such as may be designated, deposit a spadeful of earth.
6. SONG.
   (Note. Where impracticable to plant trees — shrubs, vines or flowers may be substituted. A flower bed may be laid out, and vines set in or seeds planted.)

INDEX